Wonderfully,
Fearfully
Made

Wonderfully, Fearfully Made

*Letters on Living with Hope,
Teaching Understanding,
and Ministering with Love,
from a Gay Catholic
Priest with AIDS*

FATHER
ROBERT L. ARPIN

HarperSanFrancisco
A Division of HarperCollins*Publishers*

WONDERFULLY, FEARFULLY MADE: *Letters on Living with Hope, Teaching Understanding, and Ministering with Love, from a Gay Catholic Priest with AIDS*. Copyright © 1993 by Father Robert L. Arpin. All rights reserved. Printed in the United States of America. No part of this book may be used or reproduced in any manner whatsoever without written permission except in the case of brief quotations embodied in critical articles and reviews. For information address HarperCollins Publishers, 10 East 53rd Street, New York, NY 10022.

Initial capital calligraphy by John Prestianni

FIRST EDITION

Library of Congress Cataloging-in-Publication Data

Arpin, Robert L.
Wonderfully, fearfully made : letters on living with hope, teaching understanding, and ministering with love, from a gay Catholic priest with AIDS / Robert L. Arpin. — 1st ed.
    p.   cm.
ISBN 0–06–060075–6
1. Arpin, Robert L.   2. Gay clergy—United States—Biography.   3. Catholic gays—United States—Biography.   4. Catholic Church—Clergy—Biography   5. AIDS (Disease)—Religious aspects—Catholic Church.   6. Church work with gays—Catholic Church.   7. Church work with the terminally ill—Catholic Church.
I. Title.
BX4705.A7425A3 1993   92–53906
282'. 092–dc20   CIP

93 94 95 96 97 ❖ MAL 10 9 8 7 6 5 4 3 2 1

This edition is printed on acid-free paper that meets the American National Standards Institute Z39.48 Standard.

To the people I love
with grateful acknowledgment to those
who by their generous care for me
have enabled me to know who I am
and empowered me to be a better lover
especially,
> my God
> my parents
> the Diocese of Springfield, Massachusetts
> my life support family
> Jack Miffleton
> and people everywhere who strive to be
> fully human and fully alive.

I love you very much!

Dear Mom and Dad,

Greetings from California and from "your favorite son" who sends you love and hugs across the miles.

I have written you many letters over the years from the time I went away to high school in Canada at thirteen, through the seminary years, and for the sixteen years that I have lived in California.

In fact, on my most recent visit to see you, you showed me a letter I'd written in misspelled block letters some forty years ago. It was obviously a treasured possession!

I'm writing you today to tell you about some other letters I've written, which will be published in a book titled *Wonderfully, Fearfully Made*. I am very excited and happy about the book because I believe that it will be a strong and powerful witness of faith, hope, and love to the world. That is, after all, what I ought to be about as a priest. But I also realize that you might receive this news with mixed emotions: pleased at my success and at the same time troubled by all the public attention this book will undoubtedly generate. I know that you love me no matter what and that you will support me in this endeavor as you always have. But since getting published is like giving birth, creating a part of me to live on after me and to continue touching people with love, I want to introduce you to the only grand-child you are ever likely to have.

I took the title from Psalm 139 in which the psalmist expresses faith in the God of creation who "knit us in our mother's womb" and is "familiar with all our ways." This God is ever present to us. From this God we cannot hide or run away. For in God "the darkest night shines as the day." The psalmist prays: "I give thanks that I am wonder-fully, fearfully made; wonderful are your works." Psalm 139 could be a spiritual road map of my life's journey. The path was often uncharted and narrow, branching out in different directions that caused me some anxious, fearful moments when I had to choose which way to go. I realize now that I was trying to run away from God and from my true self only to find both where I least expected to, in the deepest, darkest, and most secret places within me. Wonderful and fearful are apt descriptions for God and for me. Perhaps at some point I should give a retreat on Psalm 139.

For now the stories of my life over these last five years living with AIDS are a kind of living medita-tion on the mysteries of life and death and the necessity to choose between them. These letters chronicle my journey of faith traveled sometimes in light and often in darkness with only hope to guide my way. They tell of hard-learned lessons like the value of surrender (of going with the flow) through which God can make ministry from mistake and truth from tragedy. My living with AIDS has taught me never to take anyone or anything for granted but to use each moment as a wonderful gift in which love can be received and given. I have learned to enjoy what is and to let go of what, after all, might not be mine to control.

Along the way I have met all kinds of people from the lowly to the great. These encounters, as seen in the unique insight AIDS has given me, have taught me that the pope and the lady in the geriatric hospital, the healthy teenager and the person dying of AIDS share in one and the same humanity. We all have stories to tell, choices to make, and lessons to teach one another.

Saint Francis of Assisi told the story of his encounter with a leper on the road and called it his moment of conversion. It seems that despite his faith and zealous charity, the sight of the leper who was disfigured and covered in lesions repulsed and frightened him. He wanted to run away, but he could not move. He felt himself inexplicably drawn closer and closer toward the leper. Finally he reached out and embraced the leper. When I first heard this story I assumed that Saint Francis had conquered his fear by seeing Christ in the leper. Now I have come to believe that when he looked at the leper, Saint Francis saw himself.

On the cover of my book is an image of Saint Francis and the leper. I hope that this image and my personal experiences will inspire readers to embrace and to love the most broken, fearful parts of themselves, and to see their own faces in the faces of those living with AIDS.

Your embrace heals me, Mom and Dad, and your love renews my life. That is why I want to end this letter in the same way I began it by sending you love. On the day of my ordination a woman told you that, like Mary the mother of Jesus, you would have to share in the pain and the passion of my self-sacrifice. Little did we know how prophetic her words would turn out to be. Please know, Mom and Dad, that you also share in my accomplishments. Thank you for the valuable part you play in my ministry. Thank you, too, for the special graces that together we make possible in the lives of the people I serve, especially people with AIDS. In union with them may we give praise and thanks to God in whose image we are wonderfully, fearfully made.

I love you very much,

Bobby

On the morning of 27 August 1992 Bob's dad Leo Arpin walked peacefully into the light. His wife Jeannette and Fr. Bob were at his side.

1987

2 January 1987

Dear Mama Bill,

Happy New Year!!!
It's hard to believe that it has been fourteen years since we met on that beach in Puerto Rico. I was just a young priest, ordained less than a year and even more recently come out to myself as gay, trying to make sense of it all for the first time. You were already a successful businessman on a much needed vacation. I'll never forget how we were sipping piña coladas at a hotel veranda near Condado Beach, watching the beautiful young men, when out of the blue you asked me how long I'd been a priest! I suspected then that you were psychic; I've come to realize over the years that you are. We not only became friends instantly but by the end of the trip you had become my "gay mama," helping me from your own experience as a deacon in the Metropolitan Community Church to begin accepting myself as I was.

Caught up in the nostalgia of the moment and looking back on my life as 1987 begins, I am moved to write down for you, as you have often requested, the story of my life before we met. So get comfortable. . . .

The Indians delivered me (or so the story went until I was old enough to know better) on 10 August 1946. The time, for astrology's sake, was 2:10 P.M. DST. The world of that time was busy rebuilding itself after the mess of World War II, and the postwar baby harvest was still being reaped. I was my parent's first and only contribution to the population problem.

I must have been a pretty dumb kid since I can remember nothing of my first years of existence. So to fill this gap let me tell you about my family, especially my parents. Both my parents are of French-Canadian heritage, which has played a significant role in my life. My father has always been the authority figure in the family, a strong-willed man, proud and hardworking. He has a heart of gold but rarely expresses his emotions. The life of every party, he can sit silently at home for hours. Constantly teasing my mother or me, he is at the same time very sensitive to pick up the feelings and the pain in others and quick to comfort. Like most middle-class men of his time, his education, by his choice, was terminated after the sixth grade so that he could go to work. In the war he had served with the American forces in North Africa and Italy. He had been captured by the Germans and held prisoner in Germany for eighteen months before successfully escaping. When I was born he was still feeling the immediate effects of this ordeal.

My mother has always been the optimist in the family. According to her, everything will always work itself out for the best. Not overly expressive of her emotions, she has always been deeply loving and concerned for "her favorite son" as she calls me— that concern caused some difficulty as I grew older because of the overprotectiveness. Mom is an extremely strong woman able to bear up under strain and to take command in difficult situations. I suppose she had to be strong when, as I'm told, she heard the parish priest pronounce my father dead when he had been missing in action for ten months; she never believed it. She had to be strong to help him return to a normal life when he came back, to live in a house full of people rather than be alone with him and her new baby, to work (from my earliest recollection) in factories, mills, and shops. If I would change one thing about my mother it would be the fact of her working when I was growing up. Although we lived in a house full of people, I often resented her working outside the home.

Until I was eleven years old my parents lived with my grandparents (on Dad's side) along with my aunt and her son and daughter. My uncle and aunt with their children lived downstairs from us, which added that much more to our big family. We were a close-knit family and still are so that what I lacked in brothers and sisters I made up for in attention from aunts, uncles, cousins, and so on. Since I was the youngest child in the family, I was pretty spoiled—or so they tell me.

If any person could be singled out as playing a dominant role in my life, it would have to be my paternal grandmother. I consider myself fortunate to have known all four grandparents and to have gained something wonderful from each one. Since we lived with my father's parents for the first part of my life, and since my mom always worked, my grandmother exerted the greatest influence on me. Anyone who knew her would have to agree that she was a living saint. She spent her life working for others, doing good, and praying constantly. If God called me to his priesthood, it was certainly through the intermediary of her example.

For as long as I can remember, I've been fat. This too has influenced my life in a significant way. I've never been good at sports and so never cared to play—especially since I was made fun of when I did. Teasing and being laughed at were part of my life from a very early age, and through grammar school, high school, college, and part of the major seminary, I was the brunt of jokes and ridicule because of my size. For years I suffered through the names, the rejections, the hurt feelings that go along with obesity. Only when I began to accept myself as I was, did the whole world seem to change its attitude toward me.

I've jumped way ahead of myself. Let's go back to school. I've always been a good student. In fact, humility obliges me to admit that since college I've been an excellent student. It's not that I enjoy scholarship; I'm just good at it. I certainly thank God for arranging that. If I didn't like it and got bad grades besides I'd be in real trouble. Anyway, in grammar school I spent nine years under the guidance of the Daughters of the Holy Ghost. These were good years though I was bothered by the problem already mentioned (which had a lasting effect on my relationships with others) and by nervousness to the point that I would get imaginary pains and such. For as far back as I can remember I've wanted to be a priest. I really can't say with any certainty where the idea came from. I do know that by the time I was five years old I was playing priest and saying Mass with Necco wafers. In hindsight and with much more self-awareness, I can conjecture that a certain need/desire for respect and recognition was joined with the religious roots of family training to keep alive the passing dream of priesthood of every Catholic boy in Catholic school. This dream was certainly fostered in grammar school. When the time came to choose a high school, I expressed my desire to go to the seminary. My parents left the decision to me and so I entered St. Hyacinthe Seminary in Quebec, Canada. Those years were mixed with growth (being away from home and those who helped to spoil me) and heartache (caused by the growing pains of making friends and the difficulty of the situation in the school). If forgetting is a form of escapism from an unhappy past experience, then I certainly must not have been too happy then since I can remember very little about those years. I guess that at the time I must have thought that I was happy, otherwise I would have come home. Looking at the situation with experienced eyes, I certainly would not repeat my actions.

College, which by then I hoped would be in a secular school, ended up in St. Thomas Seminary in Connecticut. The two years of college were better than the previous four in terms of relationships and vocational understanding. I was able to develop personal values and ideas. The place was run like a prison, which still hindered my growth by protecting me in its rules and structure.

The most significant years of my formal education were spent at the Seminary of Our Lady of Angels in Albany, New York. This was the late sixties and early seventies and the nation and the world were struggling with justice and peace issues prompted by the Vietnam War. The Church and seminaries were changing as Vatican Council II began to take hold. I was changing, too, growing in self-knowledge and developing personal values. As the traditional structures were taken away, I thrived in the freedom to establish my own. I learned that I'm at my best in situations that call for independent, creative thinking and decision making.

Ordination and First Mass on 6 and 7 May 1972 are a memory blur of religious excitement and endless celebration. It's strange to look back to that time and wonder if I was celebrating the attainment of a goal or the beginning of a new life. In either case, it was the occasion for a lot of partying; and, as you know, I do like to party!

Bill, we're now almost at the point where we met. The first few years of being a priest, in fact all fifteen years, could (and perhaps someday will) be the subject of a book. For this letter it will suffice to briefly outline some significant life-directing events.

In the first months after ordination I suffered from a terrible case of "messiah complex," working eighteen hour days and feeling certain that I, single-handedly, would "save the world." I worked as a parish priest, where difficult authoritarian pastors and loving, supportive congregations soon taught me where I would get the most strokes in my ministry. I worked as chaplain to the students and faculty of Smith College from which I gained valuable insights into the feminist consciousness and the role of women in the Church. I also served on the Diocesan Liturgical Commission. At this time, I was discovering that I was gay and trying to make sense of my life. I learned about Dignity, and began a rich and active ministry to the gay community, which has continued to the present. I guess my body couldn't take all the stress because by Christmas I was struck down with hepatitis, which led me to slow down and go to Puerto Rico for some rest. That's when we met.

You already know the rest of the story so for the sake of completeness I'll just review the highlights. Maybe you'll get some new insights about me.

Soon after the Puerto Rico trip it was business as usual resulting in a recurrence of my hepatitis. This time I was hospitalized and then placed on sick leave for five months. That was followed by months of interim assignments. All the while I was still trying to balance my sexuality and my priesthood. Finally, weak and frustrated, I decided that I needed some time to sort out my life and so I took a leave of absence from active ministry.

The two years I spent in San Francisco were perhaps the most growth-filled and concurrently the most painful of my life thus far. To support myself, I worked a variety of jobs, including selling Fuller Brush door-to-door. For the first time in my life I was able to have my own apartment and to totally take care of myself. I met the challenge courageously, if I may say so myself. I was working as a chef in a small restaurant, making new friends, getting regular counseling, ministering without collar or pulpit. I slowly reintegrated my life with my ministry. With some good friends as spiritual teachers, I learned, once again, to accept, to love, and to celebrate who I am until one night on a lonely beach I was able to find the power that comes from surrendering to God. The effects of that religious experience continue to be felt.

Here's some news, Bill. I've moved again, and I'm living on 18th Street with someone named Chris with whom I went to school back in Albany in 1972. I love living in the Castro, but it's more and more painful to watch so many of my friends get sick and die of AIDS. This damned disease has the whole city crying for the loss of her sons. Sorry! I got carried away there. As you can tell, it's a subject close to my heart.

This is probably a sign that it is time to stop. I feel hugged just knowing that somewhere out there you are thinking of me. You are often on my mind and always in my heart.

I love you very much,

Bobby

FIRST LETTER TO D

*D (that's the whole name) is a friend of long
standing with whom I can share anything. She lives
in Las Vegas and is a therapist to the stars.*

St. Helena, CA
5 August 1987

Hello D, my wonderful friend!

You've been waiting very patiently to receive this
letter and to have me recount for you, and for the
record, the events that have happened since my diagnosis with AIDS in April. There is so much to tell
that I'm not quite sure where to begin. My feelings
are still too raw and stormy to sort out as I try to
deal with dying at age forty from a horrible, disfiguring, and prejudice-filled disease.

I've come up to St. Helena in the Wine Country
to get away from the city and away from the telephone that's been hounding me for days since I took
the historic risk of going public and saying on television that I was a Catholic priest who was gay and
who had AIDS. The interview with Hank Plante appeared on channel 5 on Tuesday night, and then on
Wednesday, channel 4 aired part of a sermon that I
had given at St. Boniface Church in which I had

come out as having AIDS to the Dignity community. The initial response has been overwhelmingly positive. In fact, so far I've gotten none of the predicted negative reaction and not even one crank call from an angry fundamentalist. That, I expect, will come later. Thankfully, for now all the calls, letters, and cards offer help, support, and lots of love. I have those videotapes, by the way, in case you'd like to see them.

"What led me to go public?" you ask. I can assure you that it was not any personal vanity or wanting to see my face in the media. Rather it was a growing sense from the very beginning of this saga that my diagnosis of AIDS was a gift from God. Now, before you think I just fell out of a tree and hit my head, let me explain. I do not believe that God gave me AIDS. Nor do I believe, like some religious fundamentalists, that AIDS is God's punishment on sinners. A deadly virus attacked my body and gave me AIDS. God gives me hope that can transform tragedy into opportunity. Along with the awareness that I was sick and dying came the sense that I had nothing to lose. For the first time in my life I was free to say and be who I am without being afraid. Now that is a gift! And like every gift that I've ever received from God it is a call to ministry, a call to use my life to proclaim the good news that *God loves us just as we are*. Since 1981 when I visited the first AIDS patient in San Francisco, I've seen firsthand the lack of compassion, sensitivity, and active support for AIDS patients. Individuals and government seemed to be saying that AIDS attacks only gays, drug users, and similar unsavory people not worthy of protection. In God's providence I now had the opportunity to attack prejudice and ignorance head-on. By saying publicly that I am a gay priest with AIDS I could begin to legitimize AIDS, and maybe even being gay, to the general public. How much more legitimate can you get than a priest? So when Hank Plante called to ask me for an interview, I agreed.

The only negative response that I have received so far was from the hierarchy. The Archbishop of San Francisco through my bishop in Massachusetts expressed concern that my family and I would be hounded by the media and that I would have no peace. I think it's their own inner peace that's disturbed to hear the truth that priests are human beings; that we are sexual; that some of us are gay; that we are saints, sinners, and lovers; that we can get AIDS.

Whew! I'm glad I got that off my chest! Thank you for being there to hear it. You know I love you and Andy very much. I've been thinking about you a lot in the last few days and remembering how I spent my fortieth birthday with you just a year ago. You nurture and love me and you prove my theory that we love the ones we trust. I trust you and Andy because you tell me the truth about yourselves and about me and you accept the truth of my life without question or judgment. What a beautiful gift we give one another. I hope to find ways to give this gift to as many people as will accept it. That's part of what I'm about to do with the rest of my life.

Right now I'm relaxing up here in the Wine Country. When I get back home I need to start taking care of my unfinished business. I plan to sell some things to lighten the load that I carry around with me, to secure a safe and user-friendly place to live, to write a will, to travel some, and to write and tell people that I love why and how I love them.

That ought to be enough to keep me busy for a lifetime!

I love you very much,

Bobby

P.S. I'm feeling fine. Thank God!

19 August 1987

Dear D,

I just received a letter that put me in an emotional tailspin. Actually, it was a copy of a letter that my doctor wrote to my bishop in Springfield giving him an explanation about my current medical condition. Let me quote a few lines for you.

> Approximately four months ago, Father Arpin was diagnosed with AIDS, Acquired Immune Deficiency Syndrome. The disease is viral in nature and attacks the immune mechanism to the body. This is the mechanism that fights off disease. Presently, the disease is noncurable and once diagnosed the end result is death.

Sounds pretty final, doesn't it?!!

It doesn't say anything I didn't already know, but seeing it in black and white conjured up again the whole myriad of feelings and emotions that I experienced for the first time with such intensity when I was diagnosed with AIDS four months ago.

I had gone to my doctor's office for a routine physical, mercifully put off for a month because I was to be chaplain on a cruise ship for Holy Week. (This bad news would have really ruined that vacation!) In the course of his examination, the doctor found some spots on my arm and very matter-of-factly said, "Gee, that looks like KS." As I sat there in shock, he just kept going on with the examination and suggested that I have the spots biopsied. What happened next remains a blur in my memory. Things just sort of flow into each other; I guess I was on emotional overload so I just shut down.

I remember making an appointment that very afternoon with my dermatologist who surgically removed the spot for a biopsy and said, much like my regular doctor, "Looks like KS." The next seventy-two hours, waiting for the results, were the longest of my life. I remember that I only told a couple of people and that I tried not to think about, much less feel anything over, what was going on. When I went back to see the dermatologist, I was escorted into his inner office. This man in his fifties, who looked and acted like someone you could trust, threw his arms around me, started crying, and said, "Father, I've never had to give a diagnosis with such pain in my life." Then I started crying, too. And all the feelings that I had put on hold for the past seventy-two hours came flooding in. I realized what was happening to me, and waves of fear, confusion, anger, sadness, and relief came flooding in on me, almost drowning me in feelings.

I remember walking out of the doctor's office and calling my friend Frank from a phone booth on the corner. He insisted I wait right there on the corner for him. Much later I found out that Frank was so upset by the news that instead of driving or taking a cab, he ran the ten blocks from his office to that street corner to come and find me.

Perhaps the most surprising feeling to me was relief. After more than five years of living with the knowledge that I was HIV-positive, there was a certain sense of relief in finally being diagnosed. I realize that may sound strange . . . it does to me too . . . but it is a reality for me and for some others I have spoken to who were in the same boat. Five years is a long time to be waiting for the other shoe to drop . . . to be checking yourself for spots or lesions . . . to be fearful that every cough is a sign of pneumosystis pneumonia, every tiredness a sign that you are diseased. In some strange way finally getting the diagnosis was liberating. Now I could get on with the rest of my life . . . however difficult that might be.

The next few days and in fact the months since then have been spent sorting out and dealing with all the feelings and the questions and the radical, irrevocable changes that being diagnosed with AIDS brought into my life. The strongest emotion, then as now, is fear. I'm not afraid of death; I'd be in the wrong business if I were. And over the years as a priest I've helped lots of people go through that ultimate doorway. But I am afraid of dying. It's a fear born of years of experience as a hospital chaplain watching the dying process as a sometimes painful, always draining experience in which folks not only give up their lives but their dignity and their self-control as well. I'm afraid of the disease and what it can do to me.

Since 1981 when I visited the first AIDS patient in San Francisco, even before they had put a name to this "gay cancer," as it was then called, I've watched it rape and ravage the bodies and minds of so many people, many of whom were my personal and intimate friends. I know too well how painful and disfiguring this disease can be. I was afraid of the private and public reaction to my having AIDS. How was I going to tell my parents—who for years never even wanted to hear that I was gay—that their only son was going to die? How would I tell my bishop and the Church that a Catholic priest had contracted a deadly, sexually transmitted disease? How would I tell my friends? Would they run away from me, treating me like Typhoid Mary? And how would the people to whom I ministered as a priest react? Oh God, sometimes I just wish this was all a bad dream and the whole thing would go away.

There were so many medical questions. Was I contagious? Would I have lots of pain? And the ultimate question: *How long did I have to live?* And then even more questions: If I did live, where would I live? Could I work? Where would my money come from? Who would pay the medical bills? There seemed to be so much to do, so many questions to answer, and part of me just wanted to deny that the whole thing was happening and not deal with it at all.

Within a week I began to get answers to some of the questions. My doctor said that my prognosis was about seventeen months. Now, before you get upset and start giving me the line about doctors playing God, let me say that I really trust my doctor and that what he was giving me was his best medical advice based on the life expectancy of people at my level of disease in San Francisco. However

long I was going to live, the message was, "If you
have any unfinished business, take care of it *now*."

From the San Francisco AIDS Foundation and
the Shanti Project I was able to get other questions
answered and began building an emotional and physical support system for myself.

It was from my friend Frank that I first heard
the saying: "Life is like an onion; one peels it layer
by layer . . . while crying." I've been doing lots of
crying in the last few months, trying to make sense
of what's been happening to me. But I am realizing
that AIDS, like anything else, can be a tragedy or an
opportunity. Confronted with the diagnosis of AIDS,
I do have a choice: I can either sit around and wait
to die, or I can peel that onion and choose to live one
day at a time.

Good-bye for now, D. I love you very much,

Bobby

28 August 1987

Dear D,

The reality of living with AIDS is starting to set in and there are days, like today, when my energy is very low. I don't know if the disease is progressing or if I'm just emotionally drained from everything that's been going on. The doctor says he doesn't know either so for now I just have to live with it. Which reminds me of something that happened not long after I was diagnosed.

I was in bed napping when the phone rang. I wasn't feeling very well, so I hesitated to answer it, thinking that it would probably be somebody wanting something again and I wasn't much in the mood for giving. But years of conditioning wouldn't let me ignore a ringing phone.

The voice at the other end said, "Hello . . . is this Father Arpin?"

I said "yes" and knew I'd made a mistake. I shouldn't have answered the damn phone!

"I need a priest," the voice said. "My friend has AIDS. He just came home from the hospital and he's very sick. He's asking for a priest. Would you come?"

"Of course," I said. "Give me an hour."

I dragged myself out of bed, put on my collar, and drove to the specified address. On the way I reviewed what I'd learned from the phone call. (You learn to read clues when you're a hospital chaplain.) First, the man had just come home from the hospital, which meant that, if he were Catholic, he would have received the sacraments there. So I was not being called to give sacraments. Second, the man had a serious moral dilemma since he was asking for a priest so soon after he got home. Third, the way the voice had said "my 'friend' is home" had left me wondering if they might be gay. In that case "friend" was a translation for "lover" to make it acceptable to the priest. Finally, since only a few people knew that I had AIDS, I had probably been referred to them as a "sympathetic priest."

I was greeted at the door by a nice looking Hispanic man. Right so far! I was led up to a large bedroom with a beautiful panoramic view of San Francisco Bay. In a hospital bed was a very sick man, approximately forty years old. His abdomen was distended. He was palish green. He had the pallor and the look of death about him. Pain and anguish showed in his face, and his eyes were filled with questions and with fear.

"Sit down," he said. "I need to talk."

But talking came with difficulty, interspersed with choking coughs that would leave his body shaking in spasms and with cramps that resulted in frequent runs to the bathroom. His breathing was distressed and he frequently needed oxygen as he told his story: In the last two years he'd become sicker and sicker and no one was able to diagnose what was wrong. As a physician himself, he suspected the worse. Finally he'd been diagnosed with ARC and then six months ago with AIDS-related lymphoma. But the tale of what was happening to his body and of the disabling disease that made him less and less able to function as a physician and made him more and more an invalid was not the worst of what he wanted to share.

"You see, Father," he said, "I now have a real dilemma. I am a scientist and for most of my adult life I have looked to science not God for the answers to men's problems. I fell away from the Church and became agnostic. But in the course of my sickness and through the ministry of a good priest I knew at the hospital, I was able to be reconciled to the Church and to receive the sacraments again. And now I find it's got me in a bind. I'm a doctor. I know that I'm looking forward to a long and painful death. A few months ago, before I came back to the Church, I probably would have chosen to end my life rather than go on like this. But the Church says I can't commit suicide. I'm stuck. If I'm faithful to the Church I have to spend a long time dying in pain. Help me! Help me to know what to do."

We sat in silence for a while. As I watched him struggle for breath I realized that this man who was saying that he wanted to die was really struggling to live. "OK, God," I prayed silently, "this one's yours. I don't know what to say." The words that came from my mouth were: "I think you're limiting your options." That even surprised me! But God was on a roll and I heard myself saying: "It seems that you've limited yourself to two ways of dying—long and painful or quick and easy. Either way you're dying. And dying long or short can be pretty boring. I think you ought to choose to live."

"What do you mean live?" he said, almost angry. "I have AIDS! I am dying!"

"You're a doctor," I said, "you know that dying means closing in, cutting things off, letting go of body functions. We take in less air, less food, less light, less life until we use up all we have and we shrivel up and die."

"I'm experiencing that firsthand," he said with sarcasm and sadness in his voice.

"Yes you are, but you can choose to live as much as you can for as long as you can."

"How? I don't understand."

"Open up your life and expand it. Bring into it all of the things that are around you: the chimes of your grandfather clock and the brilliance of the bay, the friends who come to visit you and all the cards and flowers you receive, all the people who tell you they care, even the pain and the drugs that numb it weave it all into the tapestry that makes up your life. You might find that instead of waiting around to die you won't have enough time to live."

There was a fire in his eyes now, a sign of the life that was still there waiting to be lived, and he said, "That's easy for you to say; I'm the one lying in this bed with AIDS."

With as much love as I could muster I said to him, "I understand; I have AIDS, too."

I can't describe the look on his face, it was understanding, surprise, shock, and questioning as he blurted out, "But you're not afraid!"

"I'm afraid sometimes, too," I said, "and being afraid is OK. That's when we need other people to hold on to us and help us face our fear. But I'm here to tell you that we don't need to be afraid."

He was getting tired at that point, so I stayed for just a little while longer. I never saw him again. Just a few weeks later I heard from his lover that he had died of natural causes, very peacefully and very alive. He wasn't afraid anymore.

I suppose I heard God's message to me that day too. I choose to live!

I love you very much,

Bobby

COMING OUT OF MORE THAN
ONE CLOSET

8 September 1987

Dear D,

In previous letters I told you how I was diagnosed
with AIDS, and how I came to be on national television to tell the world that God loves us all. I'm now
writing, as promised, to tell you the story of how,
in a few weeks' time, I told four bishops, my parents,
my family, and lots of my friends that I had AIDS,
and that I was gay. That event, or series of events,
was a coming out not just of one closet but of many.
You'd better get comfortable because this is going
to be a long story spanning more than fifteen years
of my life.

The first closet I came out of was discovering
for myself that I was gay. It was perhaps the most
difficult closet because it was the deepest. For
twenty-six years I had repressed, hidden, or who
knows what else the fact that I was even sexual,
much less gay. I can honestly say that I didn't know
until six months after ordination that I was gay. In
fact, I knew very little about being gay at all except
that gay people were attracted to members of the

same sex. It wasn't until all the effort at spiritual growth and understanding myself as a minister called to serve God had settled in and reached a high point with ordination that I started, for the first time in my life, paying attention to my physical and emotional desires. I started recognizing that I was having fantasies that weren't all related to standing at the altar and being a priest and that I was attracted emotionally and sexually to other men. You don't have to have sex to think about it and to recognize that it's a part of who you are.

This self-recognition came very slowly for me. Way back in 1972, after I was ordained, it was helped along by a series of ministries and events not the least of which was my appointment as chaplain to Smith College in Northampton, Massachusetts. Smith is the largest all-women college in the world. So I was introduced early in my ministry to the notions of feminism and, in the process, met lots of lesbians on campus. I remember celebrating Mass in a hall with five hundred people and I couldn't say "brothers and sisters" because I was the only man in the place. Not far away was the University of Massachusetts, at Amherst, which had a Gay Student Union. I remember one Saturday evening—I was the junior priest in the house and so got all the duty for the Saturday night confessions—I was in the church mostly by myself hearing an occasional confession as people wandered in from 7 to 8 P.M. Well, this one night someone came in and, as part of his confession, mentioned some homosexual activity. The following week there were two or three people. And finally, in the third week after I heard confessions, someone—a group, actually—came to the rectory and knocked on the door and asked if they could speak to me. They identified themselves as being from the Gay Student Union at the university. I asked them in and said, "What can I do for you?" And they said, "You already have. You are the first priest in this area who has not thrown us out as soon as he heard who we were." That event moved me deeply. How could a priest throw out people who were coming to seek spiritual guidance? As a young, idealistic priest, I just didn't understand it. Thank God.

It has never been easy being a priest and being gay. Still I can honestly say that I've never had any guilt and I never felt it was bad or even wanted to change it. In fact, there was an excitement about this new self-discovery. I felt that I had new ways to relate. I was experiencing feelings that I had never experienced before and it was wonderful. But while I never wanted to change it, people around me who represented the Church for me certainly did. I remember going to my spiritual director at the time, and his response to my revelation was, "You cannot be a priest and be gay at the same time." He promptly referred me to a psychiatrist. Thankfully, the psychiatrist asked me if I felt guilty about it and when I said no, said, "Good, you shouldn't feel guilty about not feeling guilty. You're not the first gay priest and you won't be the last. Just be discreet." That, in the long run of my life, has turned out to be very good advice.

Well, despite what I was hearing from the Church about not being both priest and gay, my own good sense told me that that was wrong. The theology I'd just finished learning after many years in the seminary said that I had been ordained to be a priest forever. The gay part of me, that which was brand new but very much alive, and the reading I'd been doing about this new me said that psychologically I couldn't stop being gay. It was part of who I am, like my eyes are green. And so applying the wisdom of Solomon, I realized that to survive I couldn't cut myself in two. With the oil still wet on my consecrated hands, I had to find a way to live with both parts of who I was. To find that way I turned to my old friend, Jack. Jack had been my mentor and spiritual director through most of my seminary years. He knew me perhaps better than anyone else in the world. As it turns out, maybe even better than I knew myself. Jack had been the preacher at my first Mass. In his pastoral wisdom as one who had been novice master for his community and who was wise in the ways of the world and the Church, Jack gave me advice that would last me the rest of my life. Jack said, "Bob, you didn't know that you were gay before you were ordained, but God knew. And God called you to priesthood. And because God doesn't make junk, or make mistakes, then your gayness must be part of your ministry and you'd better find ways to use it to proclaim God's love."

I took Jack's words to heart and attempted to live them having come out to myself and to God. But to survive in the institutional church I chose to be silent about my sexuality. Perhaps now since I am able to see clearly for the very first time God's action in my life through my being gay and through having AIDS I can understand how very prophetic Jack's words to me were way back in the early seventies.

So while I never really felt guilty about being gay, or that there was any sinfulness attached to my sexuality, I was keenly aware of the Church's condemnation and of society's judgment. And so while it was difficult, it was necessary to keep quiet, but not too quiet. I've never been good at keeping my mouth shut, and so I found Dignity, an organization of gay Catholics whose national office at the time was in Boston. This discovery was also a gift because, at a time when I was exploring how to get in touch with who I was, both as a new priest and as a newly sexual person, here was an organization of other people like myself who wanted to maintain their Catholicism in the midst of their gay sexuality.

I found myself traveling very often to Boston on my time off. I discovered other gay priests and that I was not the only one. And I heard stories of persecution by the Church that confirmed my need to stay in the closet. This caused me no end of stress as I couldn't share who I was and all these new and wonderful parts of me except to a few close friends. Some of these were laypeople from my very first parish who loved me very much even though they didn't understand everything that was happening to me. I had questions of integrity. It was uncomfortable hiding parts of who I was as if there was something wrong with them when I knew in my heart that they were gifts. I needed desperately to find role models, to find people who could help me be faithful to my calling as a priest and to my calling as a human being, and to balance both parts of me.

At this same time, as a brand new priest, I was suffering from a terrible messiah complex as all new priests do, and working very hard at single-hand-edly saving the world. Eventually though, I had an increasing sense of being lost in the role that led, after a few years, to my needing and seeking a leave of absence. I hope you aren't bored by now, because there's lots more to tell. This whole thing could have been titled "The Search for the Real Bob Arpin."

After three years, that search led me away from Massachusetts and my diocese and even the priest-hood and brought me to San Francisco. There I could be immersed in the gay life-style in the hope of getting rid of some of the schizophrenic feel-ings I was experiencing. In San Francisco I might be able to establish lots of gay friendships. I could seek out gay sensitive therapy. And who knew if I might even fall in love. It is, after all, a common human longing from which even God's chosen ones are not exempt.

Once in San Francisco, I discovered quickly that even this gayest of cities had closets to hide in, too. The Church was not very popular in the gay com-munity. It seemed always to be condemning, point-ing fingers, and accusing gay people of sin. The Church was always on the opposite side of efforts at gay civil rights. Anita Bryant and other religious fanatics were going wild in the mid-seventies, and so while I did tell my closest friends that I was a priest, in order to belong in the gay community I had to hide it from most people. I discovered that just telling folks I was a believer or a Catholic brought out their rage toward the Church. And so, despite my best efforts to avoid it, I found myself the min-ister again, talking about God's love and mercy and doing ministry. That is in hindsight a lesson for me in evangelization. I didn't have to be a priest, all I needed to do was be a Christian, and I found many opportunities to speak of God to the people around me. This was, in the end, a factor in bringing me back to full-time ministry in the Church.

When I did return, I decided that I could no longer hide. On a trip back to Massachusetts, I told my bishop that I was gay. He was, as he has always been with me, kind and caring. "You're not the first," he said. Although I had changed a lot, with the help of therapy and good friends and taking time to discover who I really was, the Church hadn't changed very much. It was still institutional suicide to proclaim from the pulpit or any other public way that I was a gay Roman Catholic priest. And so, the need once again, to be quiet. Yet, I lived my life in such a way that anyone who had eyes to see, could see. I was lead to hospital ministry. I ministered to the Dignity community, and eventually to people with AIDS.

I just realized that I still have not told you about telling my parents. Hold on, that part is coming!

Before I told my parents, however, I had gone to tell the Archbishop of San Francisco about my diagnosis and in the process tell him about being gay. I remember the archbishop held me in his arms and cried with me and told me that God loved me and the Church loved me and supported me. He encouraged me to go home, face-to-face, to tell my bishop and to tell my parents. And so I planned a trip to Massachusetts. The bishop in Springfield already knew that I was gay and so I was going home to tell him I had AIDS. But for my parents, this would be a double coming-out. I had tried often to tell them. I had introduced them to my gay friends.

We had gone to the home of gay couples only to have my mother ask, "When are they going to settle down and get married?" They just didn't want to hear it. Now, as I was going to tell them that I had this deadly disease, they wouldn't be able to deny it anymore.

Once again, I called on my old friend Jack for help. He offered to come home and help me break the news to my parents. "When and where will I meet you?" was all he said. And I remember rendezvousing with him on a highway somewhere in New Jersey for that difficult trip to Massachusetts to tell the folks. As might be expected, their reactions were pain and fear. They were hearing incredulously that their only son was dying. Also, expectedly, the second wave was anger, religious questioning, and an inability to understand. In speaking with them, Jack put the whole thing once again in the context of ministry. What he said to them was also intended for me.

He said that there was no one else in the country who was better prepared to speak to the world today, and tell it what it needs to hear about sexuality and God's mercy and God's love. "Your being gay and your having AIDS are a part of your call to minister to God's people."

My parents, despite their love and concern for me because I had an incurable disease, still had a terrible time dealing with the fact that I was gay. Relatives and close friends reacted by saying, "We love you, we don't understand, we're afraid," and then by pulling away from me. They seemed to be very glad that I was going to be living 3500 miles away.

When I got back to California among loving and supportive friends, I had a clear and growing awareness that for the first time in my life, I was now truly free to be and say who I am and not be afraid. When you're going to die, you don't much care who knows about you or what they know. I was tired of trying to be who everyone thought I should be. I was tired of the lies that were being spread about me as people said that "gays were perverted" or "bad" and that people with AIDS were drug addicts or sexual perverts. Having come out of the closet to my bishops and my parents, I decided it was time that AIDS and I came out of a deeper closet, which led to my going public on national news. The Church, as you might expect, was a little bit upset and attempted to keep me quiet.

But that's another story. . . .

My diagnosis of AIDS was the occasion and the opportunity to come out of lots of closets, to tell the people I loved and the Church I served that I was gay, to tell the gay community and my gay friends that I was a priest. But most important, it provided me the opportunity to tell myself that I was free, that I was loved, that I was OK. A good friend of mine, John Carr, once wrote, "Closets are not made to be lived in." I think I'm living outside of all my closets for the very first time in my life.

I love you very much,

Bobby

MY BODY

20 September 1987

Dear D,

I looked in the mirror this morning to find the KS lesions on my right ear getting worse. That scared me a little, but since I liked the rest of me that I saw in that mirror, I could deal with it. One of my biggest fears since being diagnosed has been that AIDS would leave me terribly disfigured. That fear was magnified because most of my life I've hated my body.

Hate may seem like a strong word, but it's pretty accurate in this case. I was always the fat kid, the brunt of jokes in school, the one chosen last on pickup teams because I couldn't run fast and didn't really know how to play. Of course I couldn't play because no one ever picked me. Anyway, you get the picture. I probably lost a ton of weight in my life, literally a thousand pounds. Just to put it back on again in a never ending cycle of trying to make myself be what by everybody else's standards was good-looking. I'm dark-haired, have a hairy body and light complexion so of course I've always wanted to be tall and thin and blond and hairless. Ain't it always the way?

Getting AIDS provided me with the catalyst, the opportunity to finally make peace with my body. My two greatest fears at diagnosis were to be abandoned and to be horribly disfigured by KS. I had seen people disfigured by it, the ugly red-blue blotches all over their skin, their faces horribly deformed. . . . I don't need to go into greater detail. You have seen it too! So one of my immediate fears was to be deformed. Anyway, with that background let me tell you how I made peace with my body.

It was within a couple of weeks of my being diagnosed, and I was attending a grief support group that I had started for friends and lovers of people who have died of AIDS. Since I was dealing with my own stuff, I wasn't able to facilitate the group that night, so my friend and colleague Sister Helen was the facilitator. At the end of the evening we always did a guided meditation as an opportunity to make peace, to forgive, to let go of some of the pain that affected all of the people who came to this support group. On this particular night, Sister Helen chose a guided fantasy or meditation that I had used often with the group. I just participated along with everyone else. She first asked us to go into a private space within ourselves, a little room of our own creation where we felt safe and secure, where nothing or no one could harm us. She asked us to imagine that room with a couple of chairs, a door, and a window. To help us focus on where we were she asked us to look out the window. All I saw was desert, sand dunes, death, dryness, nothing alive, just sand and heat and death. She asked us to sit in the chair facing the door and suggested that in a moment someone would come through the door. We should not plan who would come but instead let ourselves be surprised. Whoever came through the door would be someone with whom we had unfinished business. I looked at the door and waited. Slowly it opened and in came this person who at first I didn't even recognize. He had AIDS, Kaposi's sarcoma, and was so horribly disfigured with the lesions that I couldn't recognize that the face and the person beneath all of that ugliness and sickness was me. The visitor came and sat in the chair opposite me, and I faced my own worst fear. I sat and looked at my horribly ugly disfigured body and I cried.

As Sister Helen continued the meditation she asked us to converse with our visitor, to figure out why that particular person had come to see us this night, in this place. It wasn't hard for me to figure it out, I thought. But as I looked at myself and talked to myself, I realized that the scared and ugly figure that sat before me was but a symbol. A symbol of all of the years and all of the pain and all of the grief and all of the hate that I'd managed to put out toward my own body. I was shocked. It was not I who had to forgive my body for having AIDS. It was my body that was coming to forgive me for all of the years of misery, of dieting, of unhappiness that I had put myself through by not accepting myself just as I was. As I realized what was happening, the pain lifted, the fear lifted, the grief lifted. My body forgave me and I in turn forgave my body for not being what I thought I had wanted it to be.

Sister Helen's voice entered the meditation to suggest that if we had made peace we should now make some gesture of reconciliation. I stood and faced my scared and broken self and reached out to embrace myself, perhaps for the very first time in complete and nonjudgmental love. As I held myself I looked over the shoulder that was closest to me and out of the window of my room I saw the desert had bloomed. It was grass and trees and flowers and streams and beauty and life. And then, as the embrace so brief and yet so meaningful ended and I pulled away, there before me was no longer my scared and broken self, but Jesus risen and shining in life and glory. And I wept for joy.

So this morning my fear was of the disease progressing, not of looking bad. After all, this body, with all its battle scars, is the only one I'm going to have this time around so I'd better be good to it.

I love you very much,

Bobby

THE POPE

7 October 1987

Dear D,

I want to tell you how it was that the pope came to San Francisco to see me. If you were to believe all the media hype and hoopla surrounding the papal visit, then you might think that he was coming to San Francisco *primarily* to see me. It seems that the news media had decided that among the issues the pope would face in the United States were gays in the clergy and AIDS. Since I fit into both categories, I was given lots of media attention. I was even part of a news special dealing with issues in the American Church and a whole twenty minutes of prime time was about this gay priest with AIDS.

As the time for the pope's arrival got closer, I was interviewed and beset more and more often by all the American networks, by Radio Canada, by the BBC, and even by Korean and Japanese TV stations. Things got so out of hand that my friend Jacques took me to Santa Barbara for a week to get away from the phones and from people knocking on my door. Even there, I turned on the television only to see myself in living color.

Here in the Archdiocese, and throughout the United States, a small army had been making elaborate plans for over a year. The Secret Service was providing heavy security, reviewing and approving all the details about where the pope would sleep, what he would eat, where he would go, and who he would meet. There were committees to plan the papal liturgies, design the papal vestments, redesign Candlestick Park from a baseball stadium to an outdoor cathedral. There was even major construction done inside St. Mary's Cathedral to erect a bigger and better throne out of white marble for the pope to sit on.

Even though the media thought the pope was coming to see me, it took a while for the Archdiocese to catch on to the idea. In fact, my invitation to be one of the hundred people with AIDS who would be in Mission Dolores Basilica to meet the pope arrived just about a month before the event. We were instructed to gather by 2:00 P.M. at Most Holy Redeemer Church in the Castro from which we would be bused to Mission Dolores. We were made to go through metal detectors, security screening, and ID checks. It was a long and difficult wait, especially for those of us with AIDS.

When we got to the Basilica we were confronted by a large and angry crowd of protesters. Many were from the gay community and they were yelling: "Shame! Shame!" in justified anger at the homophobia of the Church. Among them was a familiar face, Leonard Matlovich, who had been thrown out of the Air Force for being gay and who was spending lots of his time and his energy now as an activist for gay and AIDS-related causes. The crowd inside was no less excited. In an attempt to keep us busy, the organizers had put together prayers and the recitation of the rosary. To his credit, Father O'Connor, the pastor of the Basilica, prayed not only for the Holy Father and for those of us inside, but for those who were outside, too. "Let us thank God," he said, "that we live in a land where everyone is free to say what they think."

I was sitting in the midst of a group of people with AIDS wearing my cassock. Next to me was an Eastern Rite Deacon who had contracted AIDS through a blood transfusion during surgery the year before. Behind me was Tristano Palermino, the president of People with AIDS San Francisco, with his lover. A few pews in front of me was Brendan O'Rourke, the five-year-old that the pope picked up and hugged. That picture made the front pages of newspapers across the country.

The tension and the excitement were palpable inside the church. Folks whispered nervously, some joined in the prayers, and some—especially the more flamboyant gays in the crowd—gave colorful and unreserved testimony to their great pleasure at participating in this historical moment. "Oh, Mary, I'm so excited I could scream!" was exclaimed in the best stage whispers more than once around us. Finally, after what seemed like forever, the roar of the protesters outside announced the papal arrival. Proceeded by monsignors, bishops, and cardinals, the Holy Father entered the Basilica and worked the aisle as he proceeded toward the altar, stopping to shake hands and bless people on the way. When he came by me, I reached out like everyone else and . . . he tapped my hand. That was it. I am not sure what the gesture meant. Was I being blessed? Was I being dismissed with a condescending "There, there . . . be a good boy"? Was I being symbolically slapped for all the attention I had gotten, much like Ernesto Cardinal was slapped by the pope during his South American trip? Or was I simply being greeted? The pope did not speak to me.

Some have wondered whether the pope knew who I was. I tend to think he did. The pope had ridden with the archbishop in the "popemobile" to the Basilica and I was assured by my friends in the Chancellory that Archbishop Quinn had briefed him. After all the media attention about the significance of my meeting the pope, nothing happened. I was not impressed, nor very excited. Does that mean I'm jaded? Maybe, like the protesters outside the Basilica, I'm angry at the pope and at the Church for their attitudes toward me as a gay person and their lack of response to the AIDS epidemic. I must say that many of the people around me were moved to tears.

I was impressed, however, by what the Holy Father had to say.

He said that God loved us exactly as we are. He told us that "God loved us if we had AIDS. God loved us if we were gay or straight. God is love." Immediately after the service a reporter asked me if I was pleased with what the pope had said. How could I not be? He had repeated what has been my message from the beginning, and I believe the message of the gospel. An interesting side note to this comes from pope-watchers who noticed that for the first time in his pontificate, right here in San Francisco, he referred to God as "Mother."

Dignity, the organization of gay Catholics, had scheduled an alternative Mass for that evening for people who were outside the mainstream of the Church and might feel exiled from the festivities of the papal visit. The Mass was to be held at the Palace of Fine Arts and I was to participate. Because they were afraid that all the traffic caused by the closing of the roads for the papal motorcade might delay my arrival, Dignity had rented me a stretch limousine. And so, after seeing the pope, I was driven in style to the Mass.

Afterward, at a press conference that had been arranged at the Mass site, there was once again an attempt by the reporters to stir up trouble. The interviewers asked me if I thought the pope would agree with me. Some folks thought my response sounded glib, but it was said in all sincerity: "The Holy Father has a right to disagree with me."

The whole thing was a very tiring experience. I could have gone to the Papal Mass at Candlestick Park the next day, but I decided to stay home and watch it on television. I probably had a better view from my living room anyway.

I was in the doughnut shop on Castro Street a couple of days later having coffee with a friend when Len Matlovich walked by. He stopped and waved and then came in and gave me a great big hug. He told me that he had been very proud to see me there among the group that would greet the Holy Father inside the Basilica and hoped that I had not taken personally all the shouts and protests of which he'd been a part. "It's important," he said, "for some of us to be inside and to tell our truth. Thank you for telling the truth."

It may take a while for San Francisco to get over the papal visit. It may take the pope a while to get over San Francisco. I wouldn't want his job for anything. It's a tough job being pope. He's got to put up with critics like me. And my job is to call him and the Church to holiness. Did I have an impact on the pope? I don't know. With all the media attention that I got at the time of his visit, if I wasn't an issue before he came, I am now, I and all priests who are gay and living with AIDS. But then he ought to be concerned about us; that's part of his job too.

I love you very much,

Bobby

15 October 1987

Dear D,

Well, I've done it again! My recent appearance on television and my going public about having AIDS and being gay has stirred up even more shit than I expected.

The Church who when I told them of my diagnosis, accepted and supported me as the Church should, with great love and compassion, was *a little bit upset* when I told the world. And so I began getting pressure subtly and not so subtly from the bishops about not talking to the media anymore. They don't like bad press and they considered me to be at the very least an embarrassment. I shook the walls of the institution that likes to bury its head in the sand and not see the reality around it. I'm honestly not out to tear down those walls. I'm not even out to change anybody's mind. But I will tell the truth of my life. So I asked the bishops if I was being silenced. They got a bit upset at how that might look, and said that I was not being silenced. I asked if I were being placed under obedience to be quiet. Again the answer was no. "Then what are you telling me?" I asked. "We are giving you some good advice not to talk to the media," was their reply. I did not take their advice.

I think it's time that we in the Church stop living and thinking in double standards and start telling the truth. Priests are sexual, priests are human, priests are gay and straight, and priests can get AIDS.

I'm taking time away from the city to think about all this, because despite my bravado, my insides were torn apart. My newfound freedom was being threatened and people were trying to box me in again. I won't be boxed in again. The freedom of being and saying who I am feels too good, and getting it cost too much to give it up. But I can't put myself in a position where I'm having to fight all kinds of battles for the rest of my life, however long that is.

Bill, a priest friend, helped me to see that last night at dinner. We were talking about this whole thing and I said that it looks like it's a win/lose situation, and I don't want to lose. "How can I make it a win/win situation?" I asked. His response, which was very moving to me, was, "Bob, you have already won! You've made your point and done it eloquently and many people will continue reaping benefits from it. You have bishops on both coasts scrambling and afraid of you and hoping that you won't talk anymore because you make them face things that they don't want to face. You have already won. You don't need to subject yourself to more pressure and turmoil. Speak when you need to and follow your heart. But don't make it a road show that will cheapen or deny the validity of what you say."

So for now, I think I've said what I need to say. Should the situation call for it in the future I will speak up again. I cannot be silenced when I truly believe that speaking the truth of my life has become my ministry now.

I feel better just having told you the story. All this shit doesn't smell so bad any more. Thanks.

I love you very much,

Bobby

COMMITMENT

2 November 1987

Dear D,

Hi again!

I've spent the whole morning writing letters to let folks know what's been going on with me. While I'm on a roll, I want to tell you about the circumstances that seemed to have prepared me to have AIDS. As strange as that sounds, still I can see a pattern and development in my life story that goes beyond coincidence . . . which neither one of us believes in anyway. Tell me if this isn't an amazing story. . . . I grow up as an only child, and from my earliest recollections want to be a priest. I go to the seminary at age thirteen, and by the time I am ordained at twenty-five, I still have not discovered that I am gay. It takes a leave of absence and my coming to California to balance my gay life-style and my priesthood, fitting it all together into this incredible mosaic. All this leads me to be a hospital chaplain, a grief counselor, and a minister to persons with AIDS.

Jack, a good and close priest friend who has known me for over twenty years and who was my spiritual director at the seminary, was talking with me about what was going on in my life. He saw God's movement and hand in all this, too. You've already heard the story about when he and I went home to tell my parents that I had AIDS, but his comment is worth repeating here. Jack told us that he saw God working in my life. He spoke about the great needs in our world for people to recognize the value of their lives and to find new ways to love one another. He talked about the specific need in the Church to face issues of sexuality and celibacy. And then he said he knew of no other person in the country and maybe the world who was better prepared than I am by background and training to ask people to take a new look at sex and love and homosexuality and see it in the context of a loving and merciful God. I am not certain at this point that I agree with all of that. Nor am I certain about my mission and ministry. But I do believe that God is calling me to use my sickness and my sexual orientation in some ministry to those who feel unwanted.

Some recent events were also setting the stage. As you know I've been job hunting for a long time and considered my position as a grief counselor with Catholic Charities of San Francisco as transitional. Whether I would be back in a hospital as a chaplain or in some other ministry was not clear, but I knew that I was being called to do something very special. I also knew that the right thing had not come along yet since despite getting interviews by some major hospitals, I had received no firm offers. Do you remember my Jesuit friend Jim? The two of you met once in Vegas. Anyway, Jim and I decided that through Lent this year we were going to get together every couple of weeks to pray the scriptures and share some fellowship. Each time we would simply sit down, open the Bible, and read whatever passage was before us. To our wonderment at the way God works, every time we did it we were both getting exactly the messages we needed. The scripture spoke of hope and life. God said very clearly, "I am God. I am in charge of my world and of you. Do not be afraid. Let go. Be at peace. It is my strength that will guide you. I will take care of you." At the time I interpreted these messages to mean that I would have the job I needed or wanted. Well, in a real sense that was true, but it wasn't at all what I expected. God has a wonderful sense of humor and is full of surprises.

By the time Lent was finished, and I left for my Holy Week cruise on the Mexican Riviera, I fully expected that I would have an answer to my job quest when I came back. In fact, there were two jobs that seemed very possible, both in Chicago. One was chaplain at Northwestern University Hospital and the other was executive director of the National Federation of Priests Counsels. Both organizations were very interested and wanted to fly me to Chicago for interviews. When I got back I went for that physical. The rest is history. . . . Spots were found and biopsied. . . . KS was diagnosed and I had gotten my answer and my full-time job. . . . It was called living.

But all those other things had been put into motion and it is interesting to follow up what happened with them. The day that I was diagnosed, 30 April, was the anniversary of my grandmother's death. (That is the grandmother who had been inspirational to my vocation and who had formed me in my most basic and most wonderful understandings of love and support and care.) The other thing that happened was that I got a phone call from the president of the NFPC terribly apologetic about the fact that they had given the job to someone else. (At this point he did not know of my diagnosis.) I assured him that it was OK and that someone else having the job was the way it was meant to be. But I did ask him for some details because I felt it might be pertinent. "You had the job," he said, "you were the one I wanted. Then at the last minute a priest that has been on our executive board for years came in and said that he had freed himself up to apply for the position. The board met and decided that we had to give him the job." The decision had been made on the very day that I was diagnosed.

In trying to make rhyme or reason of all this I came across the following, which put it somewhat into perspective for me. I share it now with you.

Until one is committed, there is hesitancy, the chance to draw back, always ineffectiveness. Concerning all acts of initiative (and creation) there is one elementary truth the ignorance of which kills countless ideas and splendid plans: the moment one definitely commits oneself then providence moves too. All sorts of things occur to help one that would never otherwise have occurred. A whole stream of events issues from the

decision, raising in one's favor all manner of un-
foreseen incidents and meanings and material assistance, which no man could have dreamed
would have come his way.*

I love you very much,

Bobby

*W. H. Murray

1 December 1987

Dear D,

For the past two weekends I've been involved in selling off a lot of what I own. For days some of my women friends Bea, Peggy, and Norma were here from Concord, my gay daughter, Len, flew in from L.A., and my friend Ken took time off from work. They were helping me sort, tag, and price all my things for the big sale.

I decided that it was time to get rid of some things in my life, to unburden from objects that I would have to carry around. With a prognosis of seventeen months, I don't really need china, crystal, lacquered wood, and silver plate. And since I've decided to move to a studio apartment, which will be much easier to care for than this large Victorian flat I've been living in, I won't need or have room for all that stuff.

It's important for me now to place my energy in primary needs, proper medical care and the right medication, an easy and comfortable place to live, and money to live on. The sale will help with all of this.

But it occurs to me that I've had to do a lot of letting go recently. Letting go of my privacy in telling the world who I was. Letting go of my job at Catholic Charities. And now letting go of my home and lots of the wonderful things that I have accumulated over the years. My friend Frank says that "life is like an onion; one peels it layer by layer while crying." It seems like I'm peeling another layer of life's onion.

Having surrendered to dying, I'm learning another lesson in surrender as I sell off my things. Why is it so hard to let go of things? I have a funny feeling that I'll have a lot more letting go to do before it's all over.

I love you very much,

Bobby

1988

I AM NOT A VICTIM

20 January 1988

Dear D,

I am not a victim!! Persons with AIDS are not victims. And I'm getting pissed off at people who are trying to make us victims. Am I glad you're there to read all this and let me blow off stream.

What set me off was an article that appeared on the front page of the *Contra Costa Times*. Over my picture is the caption, "Victim Calls AIDS a Gift." Actually, the story wasn't too bad, and they did get the message that I've accepted AIDS as an opportunity, a gift to be used. But I hate being called a victim. It makes me feel like I'm the unfortunate recipient of some tragedy that somehow robs me of any power or freedom to make decisions. I am afflicted, I will admit, with a life-threatening disease. And while that may limit the length of my life, it certainly has no power to limit, at least for the moment, the quality of life I choose to live.

It's been nine months now since my diagnosis and I'm about at the midpoint of the prognosis the doctors gave me at that time. The other day I was looking through some old papers I'd written and found one from college days about what I wanted to do or accomplish before I died. The surprising thing is that everything I had wanted back then I've accomplished. So I sat down and made up some new realistic short-term goals for myself. I wrote down the ways that every day, or every week, or at least, every month I could take care of my spiritual, emotional, and physical needs. I promised myself to pray more, to play more, and to spend more quality time with people who encourage and support my living.

Some of us with AIDS in San Francisco have begun referring to ourselves as "people living with AIDS." And I for one plan on living as long and as happily as possible. Like the song says in *La Cage Aux Folles*, "I am what I am," and that may include being a kook, a queer, or a cutie, but I am not a victim.

Now that I've gotten that off my chest, I'll say good night, I love you, and I am getting better every day.

Bobby

LOVE IS CONTAGIOUS

Our Lady of Lourdes is the smallest parish in San Francisco. The congregation is mostly poor and mostly black. I was helping out there some weekends when I was diagnosed.

The Choir of Our Lady of Lourdes
San Francisco, CA
14 February 1988

Dear Charlene,

Of all the songs in your varied repertoire, my favorite begins

> I love you, I love you, I love you Lord, today
> Because you care for me in such a special way
> And yes, I praise you, I lift you up, I magnify
> your name.
> That's why my heart is filled with praise.

As the old saying goes, "When you want something done, ask a busy person to do it." I was stuck and I needed something done. Word had come from the Catholic Health Association asking us for permission to film the monthly memorial Mass at St. Mary's Cathedral for people who have died of AIDS. It was part of a much larger piece that CHA was doing on AIDS and the Church's response to it. That was just last month and the schedule for the monthly Masses had not yet been set. No parish was designated to sponsor the January Mass.

I turned to you, my friends at Our Lady of Lourdes, and asked for help. I was not surprised when you responded with an unqualified yes. But other folks might have been surprised—the folks who told me six months ago that the people at Our Lady of Lourdes would not, could not accept me as a person with AIDS. "They won't understand," I'd been told. "They're afraid," they said. "You'll be rejected." I had not believed those folks then, and now my confidence and trust in the love that I felt from all of you in Hunters Point was being put to the test.

I've always believed that people who know hurt and pain, who live with rejection and prejudice as part of their everyday lives, either become cynical and hate-filled, or loving and holy. My experience with you told me that God and love had won out. That's why I wasn't surprised when all of you in the choir accepted my invitation to sing at the Mass for the people with AIDS.

You did a wonderful job, as you always do. In fact, the people from the Catholic Health Association were so impressed that they used your singing as the final musical tie-in for the whole videotape. God's love, which all of you at Our Lady of Lourdes parish shared with me, is now being shared by people all over the country as the video on AIDS is seen and your voices are heard singing and praising God.

To the choir of Our Lady of Lourdes, a great big *thank you* for who you are and for the love you share.

Sincerely,

Father Bob Arpin

WHY DID YOU HAVE TO TELL
THE WORLD?

Art and I went to college and seminary together and have been friends for nearly thirty years.

17 March 1988

Dear Art,

Thanks for your kind letter and for your expression of concern for me and my health. Thanks, too, for your compliments on how well I looked in the pictures that appeared in the *Holyoke Transcript.* I assure you that I have taken no offense in your question about why I agreed to be interviewed for that article. You are simply one of many, including my father, who has asked the question: "Why did you have to tell the world?"

It's because I trust our friendship and accept the sincerity of your question that I want to take the time to answer it for you and, in the process, to put it down in writing for myself.

In the first weeks and months after my diagnosis, I became increasingly aware of the freedom that having AIDS was bringing into my life, a freedom to say and be exactly who I was without being afraid. And maybe that, more than anything else, prompted me not to hide what was going on in my life.

However long I'm going to live, it was important that I spend the rest of my life living in truth.
It really was an issue of personal integrity that continues to allow me the freedom to live fully and in
peace. I also realized with the help of close friends
and my spiritual director that somehow my having
AIDS, like my being gay, had become a part of my
ministry. In a world where homophobia runs rampant, and where people with AIDS are still considered to be second-class citizens, I felt that it was
important to bring AIDS out of the closet and to
bring to it the respectability of the priesthood that
I am privileged to share. I felt it was important that
people know that AIDS affects even priests and can
affect everyone. There is no disgrace in having a
sickness.

It's now been almost a year since my diagnosis,
and since I first went public about it. Those early reasons are still very valid in my life, and continue to
prompt what I consider to be one of my most important ongoing ministries, that of telling the truth.

I want to share with you some of the opportunities for ministry that have come from my telling
the world who I am. The publicity has made me
available to other priests with AIDS. I get letters
and phone calls from around the world, from priests
who are HIV-positive or who have been diagnosed.
They're afraid; they don't know where to go; they
don't know whom to talk to; and I'm at least someone that they know will understand. They ask me for
prayers, for advice, for support, that I wouldn't have
been available to give them if I hadn't gone public.

Telling the world also made my priesthood available to the gay community. The Church isn't very
popular in that community for its anti-gay stance.

But the community has seen and accepted me as someone who was willing to tell the truth, no matter what it cost me. They've responded to that truth telling by coming to me in their brokenness and their fear. I've been able to reach out to the gay community with a message that God loves them as they are, that they are forgiven, that they are called to holiness.

Being public has also made it possible for me to share in a very important way in the life struggle of all people with AIDS. I have been able to stand up and be counted among those who call on individuals and government to react with compassion and caring for those of us who are fighting for our lives.

Since I went public, I've become a public figure on the gay religious scene. I'm called regularly now for interviews and for my reactions about what the Church says and does vis-à-vis gay people and the AIDS epidemic. I hope that I can use this awesome position and responsibility to extend the credibility of the Church as I tell the truth that priests are human. I also hope that I can witness to the gay community that one of their own can believe in Jesus.

And finally, I think, going public has been the opportunity to proclaim in prophetic ministry the call of God to the Church to forgive, to love, and to be compassionate.

On a visit to San Francisco, my auxiliary bishop said to me, "Bob, you serve a very useful purpose, for you remind us of who we are, and who we need to be." He also added that telling that truth would make lots of people uncomfortable and would probably not get me many dinner invitations.

As my friend, I want you to know, Art, that my going public is not, and has never been, a personal need to hear my voice or see my face in the media. My public revelations have been directed primarily and solely to living out the rest of my life in personal integrity.

Thank you for your concern and your prayers, and be assured that in the brotherhood that we share, I pray for you every day.

I love you very much,

Bobby

WE DO THE BEST WE CAN

Terry and I went to grammar school together. Our long friendship encourages dialogue on some tough issues.

1 April 1988

Dear Terry,

You've been on my mind a lot lately, probably because I owe you this letter and because I have resisted writing it. That fact says much about the emotional and spiritual roller-coaster ride I've been on these past few months. It also reveals a stubborn streak that says, "I don't have to explain my life to any-body."

While that may be true, I do have responsibility to share with and confide in friends, especially such long-term friends as you, when they risk sharing with me their own deep feelings of confusion as you did. So late or not, here is my response.

The only way that I can share with you where I am in my life is to tell you about my understanding of truth and freedom. It seems to me that every person has to find his or her own truth. Whether or not that conforms to other people's truths, whether or not people agree with that truth, is not important.

What is important is that each individual finds, experiences, and courageously proclaims a personal truth. Part of my truth is that I'm gay. Because I believe in a God that doesn't make mistakes or make junk, then God created me gay. It would be an awfully cruel God who would make me gay and then tell me that I was going to hell for living and practicing and being who I am.

The main concern in your letter seemed to be around the idea of commitment, and you compared the promise of celibacy that priests are called to make with the marriage vows. It's not a good comparison. First of all, nobody forced you to get married. You'll tell me nobody forced me to be a priest. True. But there was a prerequisite that I would have to make a promise of celibacy in order to get ordained. I made that promise then in all honesty and forthrightness. If I had known that I was gay before ordination, I don't know if I would have been ordained. The reality is that I didn't know. But God knew and God called me to priesthood. Later on, when the circumstances of my life and truth changed, my responses to celibacy, priesthood, and God changed, too. Priests are human, at least this one is, and I need love, intimacy, friendship, and a sense of belonging. If we lived in a perfect world where everything was in balance, we would all be in heavenly bliss all the time. However, the reality is that we live in an imperfect world where sin exists and where we need forgiving. I believe that in this world, we all—at least all people of good will—do the best we can with what we have. I think that is all God expects of us.

If, in a final analysis, it's by our fruits that we'll be known, I can say to you and before my God that

I serve Him and the Church faithfully and fruit-fully as a priest. I am not a party-line person; nor would I want to be. The marginal, the disenfran-chised, those filled with learned guilt, they are the folks I bring "good news" to. To the traditional in-stitution I bring prophetic challenge. In this role I can join with you and with so many others whose lives have been hurt by a law-centered Church with archaic sexual ethics and morality. I can stand with you in your pain about birth control. I can share the rejection of those who are divorced and remar-ried; I can speak firsthand about the prejudice of being different. And through it all I can give Praise and Glory to the God who fashioned me, and each one of us, as we are: wonderfully and fearfully made in His own image. Can you stand with me as I call the Church to acceptance, to change, and to love? Or, at the very least, can you be my friend even if you don't agree with me? Can you trust me enough to believe that I'm telling my truth as I know it and that I'm living that truth the best way I can with the Grace of God to help me? If you trust me, you can love me, as I trust and love you . . . even if/when we disagree.

Thank you for caring enough and trusting enough to ask the hard questions. I hope that my response will at least encourage dialogue so that in our mu-tual trust in each other we can both learn and grow.

Please give Bill my love and know that you and your family are in my prayers.

I love you very much,

Bob

30 July 1988

Dear D,

On 26 July, I was on the Sally Jessy Raphael show. In fact, I was the star! Did you see it? Everyone is telling me I was great . . . but I'm only listening to my friends and they are, after all, prejudiced in my favor. I thought you might like the backstage scoop about how I got on the show in the first place and what happened once I got there.

Originally the show was to focus on Lou Bordiso, a gay psychologist whose research had led him to the conclusion that gay men have a higher degree of moral development than straight men. To support his theory, he had a panel of "experts" including Father John McNeil (the gay, Jesuit psychologist who was thrown out of the order by Vatican decree after forty years of service for speaking out against the Church's oppression to gay and lesbian people), Jenny Apuzo (a former member of the Democratic National Committee, former nun, feminist, and lesbian), Father Paul Woodrum (an Episcopal priest, openly gay to his bishop and his congregation), Victor Phillips-Chalanor (a former Episcopal religious brother), and me.

The psychologist and I were flown in from San Francisco, picked up by limo at New York's JFK, and driven to a hotel in New Haven where the show was to be taped the next day. I must admit to a feeling of self-importance in riding in the stretch limo complete with a bar and a television. Reality was quickly returned, however, when we arrived at the hotel too late for room service and had to settle for a dinner of call-out pizza. (New Haven apparently rolls up the sidewalks at 10:30 P.M.!)

When Sally found out who I was, she changed the whole focus of the show. I was to be showcased as an avowed gay priest with AIDS. The issue for Sally wasn't so much AIDS, but *"your priest or nun might be gay."* In all candor I must say that I was not left with a favorable impression of Sally Jessy Raphael.

The worst thing for me was the deception that I experienced. A little while before the show started, I was invited to a private meeting with Sally. She asked me then if there were any subjects that I would prefer not to discuss on camera. I told her that I chose not to talk about how I got AIDS since I really didn't know the source of my viral attack. I also said that I would not talk about any sexual activity. (Whether I'm sexually active or not is nobody's business but mine and anyone whom I choose to be sexual with.)

Well, the program began with a ten-minute interview with me alone. You know how the AZT makes my mouth dry so that I always seem to be smacking my lips (friends tell me I look like I've been using drugs). To her credit Sally had ice water for me, and she even told the audience that the dry mouth was a condition of the sickness. In those ten

minutes Sally asked me why I had spoken out publicly, how being a gay priest was different from being
a straight priest if both were supposed to be celibate,
and how I got AIDS. I finally said that how I got
AIDS is not important. What is important is that I
have an incurable disease that calls people of good
will to compassion. I did make it very clear that I was
not a hemophiliac and that I did not get AIDS from
doing intravenous drugs. People could draw their
own conclusions, and some of them certainly did.

The audience was stacked for maximum confrontation. There were people from the local gay
community and from Dignity, Hartford, Connecticut housewives, and some ultra-right-wing conser-
vatives who had been bused in from Bayside, New
York. (Those are the folks who claim the Virgin
Mary has been appearing to them in a garage for a
number of years.) As expected, the confrontation
happened big time with folks climbing over their
seats to get to each other. Sally lost control of the
audience as people yelled out at her and at us.

One little woman from the Bayside group jumped
out of her seat, pointed a bony finger at me, and
yelled, "You're a sinner, and you deserve to die of
AIDS." The audience went crazy with her support-
ers backing her, and the gay people in the audience
objecting. When things quieted down enough for
me to respond, I said, "Madam, you are absolutely
right, I am a sinner and I'm glad I'm a sinner because I believe that Jesus died and rose for sinners
just like me. And, if you are not a sinner, then you
are no friend of Jesus."

Later on, in response to someone who said that
AIDS was God's punishment on homosexuals, I said

that I believed in and preached about a God of love and mercy.

At another point I was able to say that I was speaking out with just one message: God loves us as we are, and if we've sinned God will forgive us; that's His job.

The Bible was being used to slam me and the other panelists over the head. Someone quoting Saint Paul that sex is for procreation said: "If God had meant for men to sleep together, He would have created Adam and Steve, not Adam and Eve," to which one of the panelists responded: "Madam, you have obviously never read the Bible. Otherwise you would know that the coupling of males and females for procreation was one of the effects of original sin."

I had never been on that kind of television program before and it was interesting to see how the show was taped. It was done live but in five- to ten-minute slots which then apparently could be edited for use in different areas where the show is a half hour or an hour long. A major underlying current of the whole show was the concern over priests breaking their promises of celibacy. At one point I asked why so many "good Catholics" spent so much of their energy and time worrying about what I did with my genitals. I think that part got cut out.

Some people in the audience were kind and supportive. One woman said that she would not care if her priest were gay. The only thing that mattered was whether he ministered to her religious needs.

When it was all over, I think what moved me most was the passion of those who challenged us. They were so angry and judgmental! Of course at some level they were just reacting to the years of oppressive moral teaching they received from priests and nuns and institutional religion.

Whoops, I just caught myself sounding sanctimonious, so I guess that's a good clue that it's time to sign off. Let me just finish by saying that I survived the show without too many scars. In this most recent moment in the spotlight I was able to maintain a balance between my personal and priestly roles. I have ordered the official videotape of the show (for which I was charged $16.95! Would you believe?) and it will be available for your viewing pleasure.

On the way back to San Francisco from New York, God gave me a wonderful gift. I'll tell you about that another time. For now, know that I love you very much, and that

I'm getting better every day,

Bobby

16 August 1988

Dear D,

Do you remember my telling you about my appearance on the Sally Jessy Raphael show and how on the way home God gave me a gift? Well, as promised here's the story.

After the taping of the show I was brought by limousine from New Haven, where the show originates, to Kennedy Airport. Well, August on the East Coast makes for very unpredictable weather. There were severe thunderstorms in the New York City area. So much so that Kennedy Airport was closed and I was stuck in the airport for more than five hours walking around in my Roman collar since I had just come from the television show. The airport was filled with summer travelers. One rather large group caught my attention. They were all young high school-age people. I found out later that they were from Florida and were on their way home from a two-week trip to France. Times sure have changed. When I was in high school we were lucky to go to the local amusement park and now the kids go to France! In any case, the young people were very friendly and said hello to this priest wandering and waiting with them in the airport. One young man asked why I'd been in New York, and I said I was there to be on television.

"Oh, are you famous?" he asked.

"No, not quite," I said. "Maybe more infamous." I don't think he understood but persisted on asking why I had been on television. My first reaction was to say, "You don't want to know," but he really did. And so I said that I had been on Sally Jessy Raphael to talk about AIDS.

"AIDS," he said. "What do you know about AIDS?"

I said, "To be honest, I'm a gay man and I'm a person living with AIDS."

For a long sixty seconds there was silence. But pretty soon I found myself surrounded by a whole bunch of seventeen-, eighteen-, and nineteen-year-old boys and girls interested, asking questions, hungry for information. Before I knew it, there I was at Kennedy Airport sitting on the floor giving a basic AIDS 101 course. I shared, as I always do, the need for them to be responsible in all of their actions, sexual and otherwise. The young people were very open and unafraid to share that they were indeed sexually active. Trying not to use fear tactics, I shared with them honest information about how much at risk they were if they were sexually active with multiple partners. I was amazed to hear that these young people had not been told any of this by their teachers or their parents, especially before they left for their trip to Europe. I felt a little bit like somebody closing the barn door after the horse got out.

I said this was a gift for me. The gift was that similar to many other occasions, the circumstances of my life and the people that I meet called my priesthood out of me. The gift was being able to experience immediately the results of my ministry. The young people listened intently and asked intelligent questions. I was impressed in the way they made no judgments about my being gay. Some of them thanked me for sharing so honestly. I remember one young man in particular saying, "I've never had anybody, a minister, or a teacher, or my parents give me such straight talk about sex and morality." Later in the evening as we all still waited for the storm to clear and the airport to reopen, they all came back to me in groups of two or three or four to say "thank you" and to ask if they could hug me. One person said, "I think tonight you may have saved my life."

Despite the events of the Sally Jessy Raphael show that afternoon, I went home feeling wonderful and feeling very alive.

I love you very much,

Bobby

8 September 1988

Dear D,

Today I received a very nasty letter from someone identifying herself as a nun. She said that I deserved to die of AIDS because I was homosexual and an abomination to God. I hope she is not teaching this crap to our Catholic school children. Her letter made me angry. I would have expected more compassion and fewer judgments of someone who has dedicated her life to God. I would hope that spending a lifetime with God would make any of us more mellow. Because of my own personal experience of God's mercy to me, I am working on becoming more tolerant of others. Her letter also left me with feelings of deep sadness as I got to wondering, as I had after the Sally show, about what might drive those who disagree with me to do it with such vehemence. I sat down and tried to step into their shoes and figure out where they were coming from. I decided to put my reflections on paper for you so that maybe together we could make sense of it all.

I know that I put myself at risk with lots of people who don't understand AIDS and homosexuality. I think some people don't understand because they are, at root, people of integrity. They have a hard time reconciling how I can be a priest with all that means to them, and at the same time be openly gay with all the negatives they have been taught about that.

Other people won't understand because they will be reacting to their own hurt. They will see me as representative of all of those priests and nuns and the official Church who has told them their whole lives that they have to tow the mark and follow all the rules to be OK with God. So they follow the rules begrudgingly and now they see me and their perception is I didn't follow the rules. They are angry at me for not practicing what they think I preach. People who stay in miserable and destructive marriages, people who are divorced and in second marriages and who stay away from the sacraments, people who feel like sinners because they live together feel cheated and hurt when they see this priest living in a way they couldn't.

But the group I fear the most are the self-righteous people. They see the world in terms of black or white, right or wrong. They believe that they are right. They have lived a "good life." They have done all the right things, obeyed all the commandments and the law. For them I am wrong. And my sense is that their attack will be the most violent because it springs from jealousy. Yes, jealousy! Deep down they long for the freedom they perceive me to have and were never able to have themselves because they were too caught up in following the rules. I think I know where that group is coming from because I might have been there once myself. They have the mistaken notion of God as a person who is waiting to catch them doing wrong and who will reward them for doing right. They have a notion of a God whose love they have to earn by keeping all the rules, by doing all the right things, and by being good.

I have come to believe, through my life's journey, in a God who is love and in a love that is free. My God puts no conditions on salvation except that I open myself to receiving it freely. Grace cannot be bought at any price or action of mine. It was paid for with the Blood of Jesus and is freely given to all who believe in Him. So to the people who say, "How can you do what is against the rules?" my response is that obeying the rules isn't what saves me. God's grace is what saves me.

And it's a good thing too . . . I need all the help I can get!!!

Despite my anger and frustration, I guess I need to pray for those who disagree with me. Not to change their minds since their agreement is not important. Rather, I will pray that they might enjoy the freedom I have found living in my own truth.

I love you very much,

Bobby

7 October 1988

Dear D,

Aloha from the Garden Isle!

I'm sitting by the Pacific Ocean listening to the waves crash on the shore of the beautiful island of Kauai. There are no lights here except for the brilliance of starlight that lights the night sky. The surf is crashing. Although it's 85 the trade winds feel cool on my sunburned body. As I sit here I am remembering the many times before when I have sat by, or listened to, or watched the ocean. And I feel once again the life-giving power that the ocean brings to me.

I'm reminded of a time . . . long ago when I was first coming out . . . when I found myself sitting on a seawall watching the Atlantic Ocean in all of its power from the island of Puerto Rico. I remember seeing a ship on the distant horizon . . . a cruise ship all outlined in lights, probably with a party going on. I could see a tropical storm somewhere in the distance with great zigzagging lightning bolts, but it was too far off to hear any thunder. I remember dreaming then about what kind of life I would create for myself: free to be me, alive and in love.

My reverie transports me to another night and another ocean. I am standing on the deck of the Love Boat looking at the stars and watching the wake of the ship as it cuts through the waters of the Caribbean. It was February 1988. I had been diagnosed with AIDS for almost a full year by then and if the doctors were right, I would be dead soon. I remember contemplating the awesome power of the sea, believed to be the source of life on earth. From the sea God had taken all the elements of life, salt and sand and water and air, and breathed into them a human soul creating people like unto Himself, people free and alive with the power to create and recreate each other in the world. Tonight on the beach in Kauai, I believe that I, too, share in the power to call myself and others to be alive.

From this beach my memories transport me once again to a time and place thousands of miles from here . . . on a beach in Santa Cruz, looking out at the Pacific, perhaps toward this very place. I had come to Santa Cruz to dream, to pray, and to discover what I would do with the rest of my life. For almost two years I had been on a leave of absence from active priestly ministry searching for the real Bob Arpin and trying to bring together the different parts of me: minister, priest, sexual person, and gay man. The week before I had been offered a job, a real job . . . not the door-to-door selling for Fuller Brush or the assistant cook at the Butcher Shop Restaurant, both of which had paid the bills and put food on the table without providing much personal satisfaction. I had been offered a position as consultant in human services, something I might have been very good at. I had come to a retreat house in Santa Cruz to look at all my options and to make some important life decisions. I started the week by listing every possible option from suicide to marriage (which as I reflect on it would not have been much different for me). In any case, I quickly eliminated lots of them. By this night as I sat there on the beach energized by the stars, the sky, and the water, I had pretty much narrowed down what I needed in my life to be happy.

What I determined would make me happy back in 1977 are no different now in 1988. I didn't want to be rich, but I wanted enough to be comfortable and to be able to share. I wanted to be doing something with my life that dealt with people and was life-giving and life-supporting, and I wanted someone with whom I could intimately share my life. As I thought about it, I realized that priesthood could give me some of those things; but there was that business of celibacy in the Roman Catholic priesthood that could get in the way of my having someone to share life with.

"Two out of three ain't bad" . . . maybe . . . but I had narrowed down my whole life to three things and needed all three for happiness. So right there on the beach, I had this conversation with God, with Jesus in particular, and I said: "Jesus, I don't think it is asking too much to live at a level of comfort that allows me to share, to work at something that is significant and fulfilling, and to share my life with someone I love. Priesthood might offer me all of those except the last one . . . but it's an important one, God!"

And then, as I sat there on the beach staring out into the waves, Jesus spoke to me. I heard Him as clearly as I have ever heard any human voice or the sound of music. And what Jesus said to me was not deep and profound like one might expect from God. In fact the words and the message were very simple, like I would expect from a close friend.

"You have a lover, dummy!" he said. "It's me. I have always been your lover, and I am always with you."

I remember feeling very angry and saying: "That's wonderful in theory . . . but you're damn hard to cuddle up to!!!"

And Jesus laughed and He said: "I know it's not easy sometimes. I am after all a jealous lover. I want your heart and I need you to be mine alone. If you give me your heart, then I will give you the world . . . and anyone that you cuddle up to and anyone you touch or who touches you will be me."

Tears came as if from my heart and washed away all of the years of pain and loneliness. I felt the great arms of the Mother God embrace me, and I felt the arms of Jesus, my lover, hold me. And I surrendered on that beach and said: "I love you and I am yours. Open the doors and I will walk through them; show me the way and I will go; tell me what you want and I will do it."

And then a whole series of events in my life flung those doors open. Jesus took me by the hand, stayed by my side, and walks with me still.

Since then, whenever I give Him first place in my life, I'm happy. When I forget, I'm rudely reminded! He always sends people to love me and to remind me of who I am and am called to be. You are one of those gifts in my life. Tonight, on this Hawaiian beach, I thank God for you.

This letter has been full of memories and loose associations of me on the beach. Little did I know how in some strange way the surrender on that beach ten years ago was preparing me to trust God enough to surrender myself to Him once more as a person with AIDS.

I'm getting better every day,

Bobby

15 October 1988

Dear D,

During my visit to Kauai I gave a talk to AIDS support people and hospice volunteers. Word of the event spread quickly and on a very hot and humid night 150 people came to a non-air-conditioned school to hear me speak. I thought you might like to have a copy of what I said.

I've been traveling around your beautiful island home, enjoying being in paradise for a little while. One cannot spend any time here without realizing how this island is so small and seeing the way news gets around so fast. It would probably be very easy to get to know everybody who lives here. Our world is becoming a small island. We are increasingly dependent on each other. We cannot make it alone. We must care for one another. We must love one another.

That is after all the message of Jesus. Jesus doesn't need our love, people do. God doesn't need us, we need God and the only way we can find God is in each other. Doing things purely for the love of God doesn't hold water. We are

called upon whether by religion if we are believ-
ers, or by a sense of a higher power—whatever
name we chose to give it, or by the yearnings and
callings of our own humanity to reach out with
compassion and care to those around us who
need it. Anybody who is sick or lonely or suffering or homeless is our brother or sister. In many
parts of the world where people lose their humanity, we see the results in carnage and wars and
poverty and hunger and ignorance and fear.

There's an epidemic rampant among us that's
worse than AIDS, it's the epidemic of fear that's
grown with AIDS. There's an epidemic around us
that's worse than AIDS, it's the epidemic of prejudice that allows us to point fingers at one another and put each other in little boxes and say
"this one is gay" or "they are Catholic" or "this
one has AIDS" or "that one is one of us." Instead
of seeing ourselves as one human family we di-
vide and separate into camps. Often in the
process we hide who we really are or lose who we
are altogether. For years I had to hide the fact
that I was a priest from my gay friends. For lots
of good reasons the Church is not very popular
in the gay community. My diagnosis of AIDS and
discovering the truth of my life, that I am loved
as I am, gave me the freedom to say to the
Church and to the gay community and to the
world, "Here I am, just as I am, and if you don't
like it, too bad!" I now believe that God loves me
just this way, and I love myself for the first time
in my life.

So one of the things I need to say to all of you
tonight is wherever you're coming from and out
of whatever boxes you have put yourselves in I

urge you to do what AIDS has caused me to do.
Discover the truth in your life, whatever that
truth may be. Find the courage to speak your
truth because only then are you truly free. Some
of you might be afraid of your truth and afraid
of what it will cost. I stand here and say whatever
it costs is worth it. The miracle of discovering
one's truth is that even if nobody else agrees, you
have the freedom and peace that comes with finding it.

Many of you are presently working in hospice.
Some of you care for people with AIDS. I urge
you and plead with you to share with them the
message I share with you, the message of the possibility of life and the freedom of truth. Tell
them that they are loved, not by God, but by you.
Because the only hands God has to touch them
with are your hands. And the only heart God has
to love them with is your heart. And the only way
they will see the love of God is when they see it
in your eyes and experience it in your hugs. And
they will find healing for their spirit when you
find healing for yours. As they will find life when
you share life with them.

Hope you enjoyed it. . . .

Love and kisses,

Bobby

11 November 1988

Dear D,

I've just experienced a miracle! If I've ever enter-
tained any doubts about a God who intervenes in
human history, they were dispelled instantly when
God touched my life with healing power.

Last Monday I went down to the Villa Maria del
Mar in Santa Cruz to participate in a charismatic
healing retreat for priests. There, Father Robert
DeGrandis, a healing priest from New Orleans, led
the dozen or so of us gathered from around the
world in prayer, teaching us the power of forgiving
and encouraging us to be open to receive the gifts
of the Holy Spirit. The participants each brought
their own spiritual or physical needs, and I have to
tell you that there were some uncomfortable shift-
ing and shuffling when I said that I had come as a
person with AIDS.

While I won't admit this to just anybody, I can tell
you that part of my own objective was to find some
kind of spiritual peace. I was needing some reassurance that I was OK. While it's true that I have
survived beyond the original prognosis of seventeen months, the disease was beginning to take its

toll. You know that I have recently developed more KS lesions than before and that my energy and spirits have been pretty low. In those darkest and most secret places inside of me I think I'd even begun to wonder if maybe all of this wasn't God's judgment after all. And in that darkness of soul the miracle happened.

As Father DeGrandis and the other priests were praying over me, he was given a gift of prophecy. And speaking directly to me from God, he said, "My son, do not be afraid, let go of the spirit of fear. I am with you. You will proclaim my love to many and be my instrument of healing." And then we all watched in astonishment as my KS lesions began to disappear. You may remember I had a large lesion on the corner of my eye that the doctors wanted to radiate because it was blocking my vision. In the course of the week it disappeared. Since then, the KS lesions that covered both of my ears have disappeared completely. I only have one left on my arm, a tiny little spot that hardly looks like it's going to kill me.

This doesn't mean that I'm cured of AIDS. What it means for me is that even though my body is sick and diseased, my spirit is healed and I'm OK. I meditated a lot this week on that message that God sent me. I believe that I truly am getting better every day.

I love you very much,

Bobby

20 December 1988

Dear D,

I made the *New York Times* today. There is this great picture of me preaching at St. Boniface Church in San Francisco in front of a great big sign that says, "God Is Gay." That ought to ruffle a few feathers.

The truth is, the article and the pictures were not about me but about Dignity, the organization of gay and lesbian Catholics in the United States. I thought you might like the inside scoop on both the picture and the event. The picture was a fluke. The photographer thought he was taking a picture of me when someone in the congregation held up this sign that read, "God Is Gay." The rest is history.

The event was the exodus liturgy, or final service, of Dignity, San Francisco, to be held in a Roman Catholic church. In 1986 Cardinal Joseph Ratzinger issued a document in the name of the Church which stated that homosexuality was an intrinsic disorder. We've come to refer to that document as the "Halloween Letter." In response to it,

Dignity proclaimed that homosexuality is a gift from God and that lesbian and gay relationships can be loving, life-giving, and life-affirming.

The Church's response to Dignity was to begin expelling Dignity chapters throughout the country from Catholic space. Last Sunday night was Dignity, San Francisco's exit. I'd like to think that I was asked to preach because I'm an articulate spokesman for the things Dignity believes in. But I can't help feeling that part of the reason I was chosen is that I'm a famous or infamous person who might attract some attention. In any case, my homily reflected the pain of feeling once again rejected by institutional religion simply for being who we are. I reminded those assembled in the church and myself that who we are are God's children, beloved, forgiven, full of life.

After the service there was a candlelight march up to St. Mary's Cathedral. I, however, didn't go on the march. I had been invited on that Sunday evening to the archbishop's house for his annual Christmas party. I was standing there, cocktail in hand, chatting with the archbishop, when someone turned on the ten o'clock news and there I was on the television preaching at the Dignity service. A hush fell over the room. The archbishop looked at me, smiled, and said, "Good homily, Bob."

I have decided to abide by his decree that no priest living in his territory should celebrate Mass for Dignity. I do plan to continue ministering to that community in other ways.

I've been in the media so much this year that it was kind of nice to have the focus on something else, other than me. But I have to admit that I take lots of delight in speaking out for justice. I suppose I'm just a shit disturber at heart.

I love you very much and

I'm getting better every day,

Bobby

1989

FRATERNAL CORRECTION

*John is a pseudonym for a priest of the Archdiocese of
San Francisco who wrote to me with some concerns
about my public statements. This is my response to
his letter.*

18 January 1989

Dear John,

Thank you for your letter of 20 December
1988 concerning "fraternal correction." I
want to believe that the time and effort you
expended to write it are gifts of love to me.
In that spirit I feel the need to share with you
again the many wonders and gifts of Grace
that God continues to work in and through me.

Not the least of these is the insight that my life
must be lived to the fullest, one day at a time. In celebrating the Grace of each moment, I strive to be
constantly open to the prompting of the Holy Spirit
as the guiding force for my ministry and the measure of my love.

As more and more of my friends get sick and die
. . . as I prepare to face my God . . . as prejudice,
homophobia, and oppression take on concrete forms

in my life and the lives of those I love, I am learning firsthand the value of personal integrity, the power of personal truth, and the necessity of self-love.

And so from the rage deep within me but in the gentle peace that comes from forgiving, I speak my truth. If, in the process, some, like you, are angered or hurt, I am sorry, for that has never been my intent. But if my speaking out disturbs the comfortable, then I, like Jesus whom we serve as priests, am fulfilling my prophetic ministry. Our experiences are different, John, both with regard to the issues at hand in the gay community and, it would seem, with regard to the reaction to my ministry by clergy and laity, gay and straight. I have gotten no other negative feedback from priests except yours. In fact, a great many priests from all over the country have called, written, or met with me to praise my courage in speaking my truth. Even though some disagreed with what I said, they all supported my right to say it.

Since in your letter you state that "many priests" share your sentiments, and since these "many priests" have chosen not to convey those sentiments to me personally, I would ask you, in fraternal charity, to share this letter with them. Please tell them of my burning desire to live in love and so to grow in the understanding and exercise of my ministry, especially to those in exile. To that end I would welcome any dialogue, sharing, or process entered into in mutual respect and fraternal charity.

Upon your advice I did share your letter with my spiritual director and my doctor. Their combined wisdom not only encouraged me to send you this response but helped me to learn a valuable lesson from the experience. In closing, I share that lesson with you: Any help, advice, act of charity, or fraternal correction given in anger, frustration, or fear is useless and unproductive. Only in love can wounds be healed, peace be restored, and life be celebrated.

Fraternally,

Father Bob Arpin

14 February 1989

Dear D,

I'm sending you a revised copy of the list of people who are my life support family. These are the folks who are my primary source of love and care. All of them were friends of mine, some long before I was diagnosed. But last year I decided to bring them together. First, so that they could know one another as people and not just as names they had heard me talking about. Second, because I felt it was important that they should meet one another before they were forced together in a crisis situation over my health or well-being. Third, to give them an opportunity to reach out to each other in mutual support as they care for me. And finally, to encourage them as a group to set up whatever organization they would need to care for me should that become necessary. In short, I bought them together for me.

You may remember that one of my original fears was abandonment, and while I now trust that would never happen, I get a real sense of security from knowing that I have a team of folks to support and love me. All these people on the list are my friends,

even the professionals who are there, and they share
a few things in common. One, they love me as I am.
(What a gift that is, bringing me a sense of peace and
well-being.) Two, they all keep me humble; they provide reality checks and help me to laugh at myself.
In fact, they laugh with me. Three, they help me to
be ordinary in extraordinary ways, to see the events
and things that color my life and to accept them
without letting them go to my head. And four, they
all pick on me, except of course for my parents. And
you want to know the truth? I *love* it.

Six people on the list belong to my priest's support group. It's sort of a group within a group.
We've been meeting monthly for twelve years to
support one another's lives in the ministry. These
guys are my first line of support. They've been listening to me for all these years and haven't gone
away. They love me and are a source of faith and
strength. They are the brothers I never had as an
only child. From them I get the loyalty and devotion
of a lover with none of the hassles. They have taken
on some important responsibilities in my health
care. One of them has the medical power of attorney to make medical decisions should I become in-
capacitated. One has set up a communications
network to let people know if my condition changes
or if I need their help. One of them will preach at
my funeral. Two others will, according to ancient
tradition, dress my body in priestly vestments for
burial. One of them has offered to set up a care
plan should I need in-home or hospice care. Three
of them are pastors, three work full-time in AIDS
ministries, and one is a pastoral care administrator.
Tom, Bob, Bill, Al, Jim, John, and Jim, I relate to

each one differently, hopefully giving to them as much as they give to me.

You have heard me speak about most of these folks before, so I'll just give you a thumbnail sketch of each one on the list.

Me: a lovable, cute teddy bear, but you already know that.

Leo and Jeannette: my parents who love me even though they don't always understand me. Although they do not live close by, it's important that they still be part of my main support and that you all have a way to contact them; that's why they're on the list.

Ken A.: my gay sister; he makes me laugh, cooks me chicken soup when I'm sick, and loves to meet me for lunch, especially if I'm wearing a knotted red bandanna on my head. (I'll tell you that story another time.)

Bea and Jim B.: elders of my adopted California family. I've spent almost every Christmas Eve at their home for Mass and dinner since I arrived in California. To give you some idea of our relationship, Bea's favorite description of me is "That little shit."

Lisa C.: my lesbian doctor.

Dan C.: my friend.

Bill F.: my psychiatrist who looks inside me and tells me I'm OK.

David G.: the friend who treats me like he always did and helps me feel normal—well, as normal as is possible for me.

Bishop Joseph M.: my ordinary. He's here because he's my contact to the Church and because he pays the bills.

Andy M.: my psychologist friend from Las Vegas who has encouraged me to live from the moment I met him, almost fifteen years ago.

D: you know her! She's my confidant and someone I can be trashy with.

Larry S.: my straight attorney friend who always encourages me to keep going.

Bob S.: my Shanti buddy.

Bill T.: my gay mother with a 300 pound heart, who's been there through thick and thin for almost twenty years.

Len T.: my gay daughter who laughs and cries with me.

   We who live in San Francisco are currently debating a domestic partners ordinance. On one side of the debate are traditionalist and religious groups who define family in terms of marriage and blood relatives. They fear that the traditional understanding of family will be threatened by widening the definition. On the other side are those who are saying that family is something that people create around them for support and encouragement and mutual care. They want the law changed so that people can register as domestic partners. I can say from my personal experience that all these folks on the list are family to me. Their support, their love, their challenge, their hospitality provide me not only with family values, but with Christian values.

Over the years I have helped other people with AIDS to set up similar support systems among their friends. It might not even be a bad idea for everybody to have a group they can turn to in crisis. We all know that blood relatives are not always there for us, but I know that my life support family will always be there because of the mutual love that we share. That love from my life support family is one of the reasons that

I am getting better every day,

Bobby

4 March 1989

Dear D,

I'm feeling sick again today. In fact, I have felt queasy every day this week. I think it's the medications. They all have these strange three-letter names and I can usually only tell the difference by the color of the pill. This one is blue and white. I've tried taking it with food, but that doesn't seem to help. Sometimes I wonder if all of this medication for AIDS is actually doing me any good. It often seems like the cure is worse than the sickness.

Do you remember back when I first started on AZT? I spent two years at full dose, taking twelve pills a day around the clock. I still have the pillbox alarm clock that I used to wake me up for the 3:00 A.M. dose. Now the recommended dose is just four pills per day, and people look at what I had to do like something out of ancient history.

Thank God I didn't experience some of the negative side effects that I heard my friends and other people had to endure: terrible headaches, vomiting, and disorientation. My energy was often very low (which could have been caused by either the medication or the disease), and I did experience some

incredible mood swings. I remember being unex-
plainably happy one minute and biting someone's
head off the next. It finally got so bad that I was
actually feeling suicidal. That's really out of char-
acter for me! I'm glad I knew that it was one of the
side effects of the medication so I could compen-
sate for it. More recently I have begun to experience tingling and/or pain in my legs. I'm told that
it is something called neuropathy and may be yet
another side effect of the AZT. If it continues I
may have to stop taking it for a while. It's scary to
think that some medicine may be keeping the AIDS
virus quiet but also hurting some healthy parts of
me. It is a dilemma. Is AZT a blessing or a curse?
To be honest, some days it's hard to tell.

I guess I have been very fortunate not to have
been hospitalized with PCP (pneumosystis carinic
pneumonia). My doctor has prescribed monthly
treatments of aerosol Pantamedine as a prophylac-
tic to prevent my getting it. The treatment consists
of inhaling this medicine through a machine for
half an hour or so. It tastes like you are sucking on
a lead pipe. Not much fun!

I've just read what I have written so far and have
reached the conclusion that this letter isn't much
fun either. Please believe that all is not as bad as it
sounds. There are days or weeks like this one, when
I'm sick every day, that cause me to wonder what
it's all about. In the shower this morning I said to
God (I do talk to God when I'm in the shower), I
said, "God, if it's going to be this bad every day and
I'm going to be sicker than the day before, then
won't you please come and get me? I've paid my
dues, I've done my thing, I'm getting tired." God

didn't answer me in the shower. Now, in the middle of the afternoon, I'm glad . . . otherwise I probably wouldn't be writing you this letter.

Oops! I've got to run; my stomach is doing somersaults again. I love you, and your love is the best medicine I can have. This letter notwithstanding,

I am getting better every day,

Bobby

Ash Wednesday 1989

Dear D,

Today I got a wonderful and unexpected surprise. A deliveryman brought a big box to the door. When I opened it, inside was a beautiful butter-soft leather jacket all lined in fur and a card that said simply, "Happy Lent, enjoy. Dan."

Now, Dan is someone I've never met. Last year, when I was on television and in the news, he saw me and began sending me cards and letters assuring me of his concern and his prayers. But this morning, that concern took on practical, hands-on dimensions. I love surprises, and this was certainly a surprise. Somehow things like this are better because they're unexpected and come from unexpected sources.

My reaction to the extravagance of a fur-lined leather jacket was to tell myself: "I'm worth it." I had to put aside the feeling of hurt that a total stranger could be making me feel so wonderful when at times my family seems so distant. I simply wanted to enjoy the moment and the feeling of being cared for. I'm going to start praying for cold weather so that I can wear it.

Oh, and in case you're wondering, though the fur looks like mink, the label inside says opossum, so wearing it won't be politically incorrect.

I love you very much and

I am getting better every day,

Bobby

1 May 1989

Dear D,

I was on my way to catch a bus the other day when this really cute guy was walking in the same direction about a half a block ahead of me. He was just the type I like, young, short, blond, wearing a pair of shorts—very tight shorts. Naturally he caught my eye and as I was admiring that side of him, praising God for giving me eyes to see such beauty, something in his hand caught my attention. It was a rosary. He was saying the rosary. Now you know that you're liable to see many strange sights on the streets of San Francisco, but this one surprised me and got my attention.

In fact, it would seem that in the last few years of my living with AIDS, Mary has gone out of her way to get my attention. You may remember my telling you about the healing retreat I was on just a few months after I was diagnosed. It was at that retreat that the priest who was giving it shared a prophecy with me, part of which said, "Mary, my Mother, has interceded for you. You have nothing to fear." I have thought of those words many times since then, wondering what they meant. Why would Mary intercede for me? I was certainly being healed. God was active in the making of my history and somehow I was being told that it was through the intervention of Mary, the mother of Jesus.

A full six months later, my friend Michael went on vacation to Italy, and he came back bearing gifts. I remember him saying, "Bob, you know I'm not very religious, and I hope this is appropriate. I saw it and immediately thought of you." His gift was a beautiful handmade cameo of Mary. Once again I was being nudged into awareness. But it wasn't until a full year later on a trip to Italy myself that I was knocked over the head and told to pay attention. The way it happened was that while in Rome I was saying Mass at many of the major churches and basilicas. I would present myself as a priest and just ask them if I could celebrate Mass. On every occasion I was assigned to an altar dedicated to Mary. That had to be more than coincidence.

When I got home, I was prompted to pick up a book that had been given to me within weeks of my diagnosis by my good friend Jack. Jack, you'll remember, was my priest friend who came home with me to tell my parents that I had AIDS. On that trip he opened the trunk of his car, took out a book that he had been reading, handed it to me, and said, "Here, this might be helpful sometime." Well, in the two years since then the book had rested in boxes and on my shelf and even moved with me once or twice. But now I picked it up and read it. It helped me to better understand why Mary was interceding for me.

Growing up Catholic and having spent twenty-one years in various seminaries and Catholic schools, I had been exposed to Marian devotion. Mary had been depicted as the pure and spotless virgin, the humble handmaiden from Nazareth, the obedient milk-toast person that as I got older I had rejected. But in *Miriam of Nazareth* I discovered the Mary who was a loyal daughter of Israel, who like Esther and Ruth and Naomi and Miriam, the sister of Moses, was a prophet and a strong leader. This Mary was someone who in her life and by her deeds bore witness to the presence and reality of God. This Mary was the instrument of salvation who let God's Word live in her and grow in her and take flesh from her.

Well, you can see why this Mary would be someone with whom I could identify in my situation as a gay man and a person living with AIDS. In both cases I had had to learn about the power that comes from choosing not to be a victim. I had had to move from the exile of being different to the belonging of being at home with myself. I began to understand that as prototype of the Church since Vatican II, Mary was not institutional religion but mystical reality, the place where God takes flesh and is experienced.

Well, I started praying the rosary again and to meditate on those events in which God intervened in history to make the power and beauty of ordinary things visible. I began praying before icons of Mary, she who in that traditional form always points the way to Jesus. Has it changed my life? You bet it has! It's gotten me in touch with the feminine in me. I've been able to wear the cassock proudly and use it as a tool saying to folks, "Take a look here, there's more than meets the eye." I'm learning to receive love, affection, and the care of others as well as be a giver and a doer. I've been able to trust the intuitive in me and to celebrate faith in the heart and not the head. And finally, I have learned that prophetic witness can be given in silent, patient, trust-filled waiting for the God who will always keep His promises. And you know what? I'm talking much more with my mom now. We seem to be getting along even better than ever before. People, places, and things have called me to pay attention to a deeper reality, to a beauty that is in each of us and in all of creation.

The young man with the rosary was certainly beautiful. Now I wish I had spoken to him.

I'm getting better every day,

Bobby

I MISS OUR FRIENDSHIP

Carmine is a classmate from seminary days. When we met at a class reunion his obvious distance prompted me to send this letter.

4 July 1989

Dear Carmine,

It was good to see you a couple of weeks ago at the reunion and to share your pride in being the first of our class to be elevated to Monsignor. You seem to be enjoying the role.

Seeing you caused me to remember our seminary days and to feel again the warmth of the close friendship we shared. I was remembering the hours we spent together sharing our hopes and dreams for our vocations and talking late into the night about the people we would serve. I laughed when I remembered how I would come into your room and get you and your roommate arguing . . . and then go back to my room and listen to the fight through the wall. I recalled the many crises we faced together through that seminary experience, all the retreats we shared in which we prayed for God's guidance in making our vocational decisions, and I remembered how we participated in each other's First Masses.

But I'm writing this letter to tell you that seeing you at the reunion also made me sad. It reminded me of the look I saw on your face on that
day when, in friendship, I had reached out to you to
share the news that I was gay. It reminded me of
the distancing in our friendship since that time.
Your "Hail-good-fellow-well-met" attitude is a
painful reminder of how far apart we have become.
At the reunion you never even asked me how I was
feeling. This seeming lack of personal interest has
left me sad and disappointed. It's not because I need
or even want your approval, but because I really enjoyed our friendship. And, as I get ready to face my
God, friendships and love are very important to me.

Most of the guys at the reunion were supportive
and caring and their love was a source of strength
and encouragement. A few, like yourself, reacted to
me with distance and silence. Since you haven't told
me how you feel, I'm left only with the silence to interpret. I choose to interpret it as fear because it's
easier to deal with your being afraid of AIDS than
with your not loving me. If your fear prevents you
from reaching out to me in friendship or compassion, then I ask you please to pray for me. I pray
for you and for all the guys who traveled with us
on the road to the priesthood.

In the power of the priesthood that we share,
may our ministries be fruitful, our lives happy, and
our deaths peaceful.

I'm getting better every day,

Bob

4 July 1989

Dear D,

Happy Independence Day!

I'm spending a quiet holiday at home. The fog is rolling in early, making it cold and damp. Typical San Francisco summer! It's a good day to catch up on my letter writing.

Since you were asking about my relationship to the Church and how it is treating me these days, I thought that I would tell you about my most recent visit with my bishop in June.

"I know all this must sound crazy," I said. "If someone had told me, two years ago, what I'm telling you now, I would probably have thought he was nuts!"

I was sitting with Bishop Joseph in his parlor. The setting was formal, but the interaction was warm and inviting. I was using the opportunity of a trip to Massachusetts to visit with him and to keep him informed about the current status of my health and ministry. As we talked, my memory brought me back to the many times that I'd sat in this room before, always to see "The Bishop," whether this man, who is always so kind to me, or his predecessor, with whom there had been conflict, anger, and a parting of the ways. In this room I had announced to Bishop Christopher that I was taking a leave of absence and moving to California. Here, too, I had faced his anger at my two-year absence when I returned for my grandmother's funeral. My trust in the power of God's love had resulted in transforming that anger to mercy and forgiveness. In this very same room I had first told the new ordinary, Bishop Joseph, that I was gay. And here I experienced, for the first of many times, the kindness and compassion of this very priestly bishop. It was here that he held me in his arms when I told him I had AIDS and assured me of his love and support as well as that of the Church.

I reflected on how that support had been more than words. After more than twelve years of my working away from Springfield, the diocese had, without hesitation, mobilized to help me. I was put on diocesan salary, assured that all my medical expenses would be paid "for the very best medical care available." And, when my physician thought that I would do better to live independently, sufficient money was provided for rent and utilities. "You have enough to worry about now," I was told. "Money should not be a source of stress for you"—and it never has been.

I have maintained personal contact with the bishop by visits, phone calls, and letters. A priest from the bishop's staff was assigned as liaison to help me deal with any needs or problems that might arise. Special arrangements were made with the diocesan insurance carriers for prompt reimbursement of the copious medical bills that are part of living with AIDS. Bishop Joseph even calls my parents regularly to encourage and support them. At first, my father was reluctant to visit with him, but now he looks forward to their get-togethers.

It was on just such an occasion, I guess in this same room, that something happened that revealed to me just how the Holy Spirit was working in my life and in the Church. My mother told me the story without quite understanding all the implications of what she shared. It seems that on one of my parents' visits with Bishop Joseph, my father was expressing his dismay at my public self-revelations. "I don't care what Bob does, but why does he have to tell the world?" Bishop Joseph's response tells the story. "I asked myself that same question when Bob went public on television and in the newspapers. In fact, at one point I even tried to stop him. I was afraid that the media might use him to attack the Church. But when he seemed determined to tell his story, I decided that I had better listen with my heart. Bob believes that his story is somehow part of his ongoing ministry now. And, if his telling it is from the Holy Spirit, I can't get in the way."

All these things went through my mind as I sat there chatting with the bishop.

Isn't it funny how we can think and do so many things at the same time and in what seems like an instant? My opening statement was still ringing in the air: "I know this is going to sound crazy, but . . . "

Well, it sure sounded crazy to me. Here I was, a gay priest, dying of AIDS, telling my bishop how the Holy Spirit was using me as an instrument of healing; how people rested in the Spirit (that's the phenomenon of folks falling to the floor) when I anointed them; how some were cured of physical, emotional, or spiritual disease through my prayer; how I felt God was calling me to a ministry of healing!! The whole thing was crazy and I was scared and trying to run . . . I had faced being gay in a homophobic church, having AIDS, going public, even death. But this was too much! I could not face being a Catholic Catherine Culman, and I was looking for someone—my bishop—to tell me what I wanted to hear: that it was crazy.

With all the evidence I have ever had of both God's action in my life and God's sense of humor I should have known better than to try to run away. Why did I take so long to see what God is doing in me? Why was I still afraid? Maybe God talks too softly, in gentle whispers too faint for my hard head to hear. Or maybe I hear and can't believe that God would use me for his purposes and to mediate his love.

Anyway, there I sat, in this room filled with memories, wanting desperately for my bishop to agree with my assessment of crazy. "It sounds to me like you're hoping I'll tell you to stop," he said. And with a smile, added, "Isn't it wonderful that God would give you this consolation at this time in your life and ministry?"

Well, there it was. I had no place to run. Now God had totally ceased being subtle with me. She had hit me on the side of the head and said: "Pay attention!" Once again God was speaking to me through my bishop, saying: "It's what I want. . . . Go for it!"

We spoke of many other things that afternoon in the bishop's parlor: money, my funeral, my parents.

But what struck me the most was God shouting to me in gentle whispers: "I'm not through with you yet . . . follow me . . . again!"

Three days after my visit with the bishop, the Diocese of Springfield held its annual celebration of priesthood, and all the priests of the diocese gathered for Mass with the bishop at the cathedral church. During that Mass Bishop Joseph surprised me by giving me the Anointing of the Sick in union with all the priests of the diocese in order to "show Bob our fraternal love and concern for him in hope and in prayer."

A week later a priest friend sent me a clipping from the diocesan newspaper with this quote from Bishop Joseph:

> The experience of losing a loved one is always a great sorrow. When the dreadful illness of AIDS is the cause of death, there are additional dimensions of grief. As Catholics and Christians, it is important for us to stand by those suffering from this disease—to minister with Christlike compassion to AIDS victims and their families—to bring the power of prayer and the virtue of hope, especially to those who feel alienated and alone.

The Church, as you can see, is treating me just fine. God is using me, despite my protests. I'm discovering new freedom in surrendering to God's will and to my wonder,

I'm getting better every day,

Bobby

15 July 1989

Dear D,

If I were superstitious I would have interpreted the negative start of this trip as a bad omen. For once I was ahead of myself and packed a full two days before departure. But I had to be compulsive and clean my desk the night before leaving . . . throwing my plane ticket away with the garbage. By the time I found it, I'd missed the plane, and the trip across the country took twelve hours on standby hops instead of six hours direct.

Once I got there, however, God began to work through me in very powerful ways.

I want to tell you about a Mass I celebrated after arriving on the East Coast. It was at my friend Ken's, a person living with AIDS who is a student at Harvard Divinity School. Ken had let it be known at Harvard Divinity as well as among some of the AIDS organizations that I was going to be in town and that I would be celebrating a home Mass that evening. Well, word got out and about a dozen or so people showed up for the Mass. For some, this was an entirely new experience, and I must admit the healing part was still fairly new for me. Remember, I was on my way home to try to talk to my bishop and have him tell me to stop doing this. I was experiencing a call to a type of ministry that scared me. And while I felt compelled to use the gift I was given, I was afraid of it.

The Mass was very informal. We sat on the living room floor at Ken's house and after spending some time in forgiving and praising God, we opened our hearts and our minds to the Holy Spirit. Some people shared scripture passages as they were moved to do so, and other people shared what they heard God saying to them in those passages. Overall the message became clearer and clearer. God was with God's people. God's power brought life and peace and healing. We should not be afraid.

After communion everyone sat back and I was moved to invite them to open their lives and their hearts to the miracles that God wanted to work. And miracles started happening. People were given dramatic physical healings, one from AIDS-related meningitis. People who had been estranged from the Church or from God for a long time were brought home. People were given new fervor in prayer. One man said that he experienced a healing with the relationship to his mother. Ken told me later that the healing was indeed followed up in reality in the man's life.

What all of that said to me—since whenever God uses me to bring a message to other people I'm the one that most needs to hear it—was that I shouldn't be afraid and that I should trust in the power of God working in and through me. I guess I needed some reassurance that I was OK and it would seem that God used this healing gift to tell me that I was indeed OK in His eyes. If the gift continues then as people need it, their need will call it out of me. The Healing Mass at Ken's was a significant part of my journey. It helped me to trust and believe not only that God loved me as a person with AIDS but that God loved me enough to use me powerfully as an instrument of His forgiving, healing, and reconciling love.

I'm getting better every day,

Bobby

5 September 1989

Dear D,

This Labor Day weekend I experienced for the very first time the status of being a hero. I must admit that I was left with feelings of humility and awe from the experience.

Dignity, the gay Catholic group, was meeting for its national convention in San Francisco over Labor Day weekend. On that particular Sunday I was scheduled for the major Mass at St. Mary's Cathedral. As you know, my celebrating Mass at the Cathedral has been for me one of the positive reactions to my deciding last year, when Dignity was put out of Catholic space by the archbishop, to abide by his decree that no priest living in his territory should celebrate Mass for Dignity. Having obeyed that command, to the letter of the law if not the spirit, I remained in good standing and was welcome to celebrate Mass within the Archdiocese and specifically at the Cathedral Church where I could proclaim to the hundreds of people gathered at this magnificent structure from all over the world the goodness and mercy of God, especially to me and other people who were gay or living with AIDS.

On this particular Sunday, I remember beginning my homily by telling the congregation that I was spending the weekend with five hundred of my gay brothers and lesbian sisters. Some of the folks from the convention who had come to that Mass nearly fell over hearing me freely say this from the pulpit of a Catholic Cathedral.

Anyway, what I really wanted to tell you about happened later on that day over lunch. I was sitting at a table with Father John McNeill and Father Bernard Lynch. Both of these men are my heroes. They have both paid their dues, and paid dearly, for proclaiming fearlessly that they are gay priests and for ministering openly to the gay community, encouraging people to live fully in faith and love. For each of them the price has been different but equally costly. John McNeill was put out of the Jesuits after forty years for saying that the "Halloween Letter" of Cardinal Ratzinger was mean-spirited and unChristlike. Bernard Lynch, who worked with people with AIDS in New York City, was falsely accused of child molestation in an attempt to stop his ministry of love and outreach to the gay community. Over lunch, John and Bernard and I were discussing how I had survived and continued to be in good standing with the Church when they were both in trouble. We had all agreed that it was probably because I had gone public and received public sympathy for being someone with AIDS. My message was no different than theirs. Like them I had come out publicly about being gay and said that God loved me and all people that He had created just the way we were.

While we were at the table having this serious discussion, some people from the convention began coming to the table to say hello. I expected them to be coming to greet Bernard or John and was surprised when they came over to me saying, "Father Arpin, thank you for telling the truth. Thank you for standing up and not being afraid to say who you are. Thank you for saying that God loves us."

It began to dawn on me slowly that I was experiencing the status of my heroes. I was being put into the same category with the two men at the table who, in my opinion, were examples of courage and truth to me and to the world. Once I realized what was happening, I felt very little and very awed. Little because I don't measure what I'm doing as very special. Unique, maybe. But I'm just saying who I am and being who I need to be. Awed because I realized the great responsibility that is expected from any of us, who, like it or not, get put on a pedestal. That pedestal, I'm finding, can be a very isolated and lonely place because those who agree with what you've done look to you for example and keep you at arm's length as someone special, while those who disagree have clear opportunities to take shots at you. On the other hand, not to be an example is perhaps in scriptural terms "to hide your light under a basket" and not to "let it shine for everyone to see" as Jesus commanded.

At the beginning of this year I had been interviewed by German National Radio. The Germans, it seems, had put together a whole program about me using quotes from some of my media interviews and gathering a panel of German theologians to discuss the intricacies of a priest proclaiming openly that he was gay and had AIDS. As part of the program, they planned to have a direct hookup by telephone with me so that I could answer some of their questions live on German radio.

I remember asking the German reporter why I would be of interest to the German people. In response he said, "You may not realize it, but you are known in Europe and around the world right now." And I said, "Other priests have AIDS," and he said, "Yes, but very few are willing to take the risks, not only of saying that they have AIDS, but that they are homosexual in the way you do with real assurance that you are loved by God and that everything is OK. That willingness to take those risks is what makes you news." Maybe what it takes to be a hero is to be willing to take the risk of being known for who you are and for telling the truth. John McNeill and Bernard Lynch do that, and they are my heroes. I'm awed that God could use me to perhaps inspire other people to discover and speak their truth. I pray that God will help me to be a living sign of His power and love.

But please, whatever you do, don't treat me like a hero. Treat me, rather, like a friend.

I'm getting better every day,

Bobby

MY ANGEL

*Gus arrived at my door on the weekend I was
diagnosed and stayed in my life for a few months,
helping me through the initial crisis. Then he
left as mysteriously as he had come. Two years later
I heard that he had died. I wrote him this letter
to say good-bye.*

Heaven 77777
22 October 1989

Dear Gus,

I just got back from the park in San Jose where a
group of your friends held a memorial service for
you. I'm writing this because I need some way to
say good-bye and to tell you what you meant in my
life. I know that you are fine where you are, but as
I sit here writing I am the one who is sad at the
death of a friend. I'm disturbed that I did not even
know you were sick. And so I could not be there to
encourage and support you in the same way you
cared for me so wonderfully in those first days after
my diagnosis.

On the way to San Jose I was thinking about that
first time we met, how, in fact, you appeared at my
door like a guardian angel out of nowhere. I was

sitting at home with a group of friends who were commiserating with me over the fact that I had just been diagnosed two days before. There was a knock on the door. It was you. You said your name was Gus (a pretty unlikely name for an angel) and that Dave A., a mutual friend, had suggested that you and I should meet and that we would probably like one another. On that recommendation, you had stopped by. At first it seemed like you would have no idea what was going on. The focus of the conversation had shifted when you as a stranger had entered the room. The topics were kept light and impersonal until you directed the conversation and began asking me some very deep and personal questions like "Who do you love?" and "Have you told them?" "What is really important to you?" and "What do you want out of life?" All of a sudden the news of the diagnosis and all of the fears and the uncertainties and the questions came to a head and I felt like somehow I was in this strange episode of "The Twilight Zone." I remember stopping you and asking, "Who are you? Why have you come here?" And you very gently looked at me and said, "Who I am is not important. Why I'm here is because I know that you're sick and I have a message for you . . . and the message is *you don't need to be afraid.*"

In the weeks and months that followed that fateful Sunday you taught me lots of lessons about living and dying. I never really did know much about you. In fact, at the memorial service it was very interesting to see you through the eyes of all of those people who loved you and to hear that I wasn't the only one to whom you had reached out with unselfish love. All you ever told me was what you thought I needed to know about your own journey, about being abused as a child, about your terrible accident that had left you partially disabled, about your struggle through doubt and fear and pain, and about your decision to choose life. Of all the lessons I learned from you, maybe the most important for me was the day you said to me, "Don't be afraid to ask for what you want. If you don't ask, you'll never get it."

Maybe, except for my grandmother, no one else in my life has ever loved me with such unconditional, unselfish love as you did. If I needed something you were there to do it, going grocery shopping, washing the kitchen floor, or just listening to the many doubts, questions, and fears of those first few months of crisis. When I was scared and lonely you'd be there to hold me through the night and to tell me that everything would be OK. In those first dark and fear-filled days of my diagnosis you were truly my guardian angel, showing me the way through the maze of emotions, holding my hand, and encouraging me and walking with me toward the choice for life.

And then as suddenly and unexpectedly as you arrived, one day you were gone, leaving no forwarding address, no way to contact you. You left only your love with me and really took little or nothing in return.

Today your friends gathered formally to remember you and to bid you farewell. It warmed my heart to hear that before your death you had made a reconciliation with your family and that you had died in peace. I want you to know that I, too, live in peace now, inspired in many ways by your guidance for a very short and significant part of my life. I look forward to holding you again and walking with you in the light. Thanks for your love and good-bye, my angel, until we meet again.

Bobby

Thanksgiving 1989

Dear D,

I could have died last night, or I thought I could. On this Thanksgiving eve I was the turkey. In an effort at economy and ease I nuked some leftover seafood pasta for dinner. About 10:30 the cramps started, followed closely by diarrhea and vomiting. And my head felt like it would split in two. I recognized the symptoms. It was ptomaine. How ironic, I thought, I've out lived my prognosis with AIDS by over a year only to die from bad clams!

I called my friend Dan, deciding that at least I wouldn't die alone. I thought about all the times when I've been so sick that I wanted to die and about all the efforts I've made in the last two years to surrender and let go. But now faced with what I thought was the real thing, I was fighting like hell to live. I guess I haven't fully surrendered yet.

When Dan got here we called my doctor who said there wasn't much to do; that it had to run out its course; and that I really wasn't in much danger at all. What I was was sick and miserable and scared.

Dan stayed with me and after a long time I finally fell asleep in his arms. The next morning I woke up in that same position, sleeping in Dan's arms. He hadn't wanted to move and risk waking me up. What a friend! I don't think I'll be able to eat much turkey dinner today, but I do have much to be thankful for. First, there's fight left in me and that's something to celebrate. I'm thankful for the preciousness of my life. And I'm thankful most of all for my friends. Friends like you who listen to all this stuff and like Dan who see me though.

There is a time, says Ecclesiasticus, for everything under heaven. Last night was not the time for me to die. Today is the time for me to give thanks.

I'm getting better every day,

Bobby

18 December 1989

Dear D,

I made it. . . . I finally made it! Last Sunday I was on the cover of *Image* magazine. The photo shows me standing before the stained-glass windows of St. Mary's Cathedral. I am wearing beautiful red vestments that were made by my friend Len. The article is a long and sensitively written story about me and my ministry to the gay and AIDS communities in San Francisco. I think it was Andy Warhol who said that everybody gets their fifteen minutes in the spotlight. In the last three years I've had more than my share of the spotlight.

Most people would be thrilled to grace the cover of a nationally distributed magazine. It is, in many ways, a unique moment of glory, a day in the sun, most often connected to fame and fortune. My ego would love the idea that I was famous for my gorgeous body or my musical talent, or even for making a lot of money in smart business deals. There is a very human part of me that wishes I were the sexy cover boy on *Drummer*. (In case you are wondering, that would be the gay equivalent of a *Vogue* cover girl.) Therein lies for me the irony in all this.

The cover of *Image* magazine says: "Bob Arpin, Catholic priest with AIDS." I don't think there is any glory in being sick, any glory in having caught a deadly virus, and certainly any glory in facing a premature death. There is no individual or personal glory in being a priest. In fact, I share that distinction with 55,000 other Americans. As to being gay, well . . . we are everywhere in greater numbers than anyone inside or outside the Church is willing to admit to. Being a gay man does not make me special . . . though being an outrageous queen might!

I can only hope that my moment of glory comes from *how* I am living as a gay priest with AIDS. I want to be famous for living one day at a time. I want to be known for the hope I offer to my friends who sorely need hope in the midst of all the dying. I want to be remembered for forgiving the prejudice and homophobia of society and of the Church. I want people to recognize me because I tell the truth about who I am and because I try not to be afraid.

The phone has already started ringing off the wall. Phil Donahue called again last night to try and get me on his show. I'm in demand again . . . the price of fame . . . and being a cover boy.

Have to run . . . Busy . . . Busy . . . Busy. It's not easy being pretty!!

I'm getting better every day,

Bobby

1990

4 January 1990

Dear D,

People I run into on the street often tell me how good I look, a desirable compliment to receive anytime but especially as I'm now into my fourth year of living with AIDS. And, in fact, I do look pretty good for someone who was told he'd be dead over two years ago! But appearances aren't always what they seem and looking good and feeling good aren't always the same, as anyone living with AIDS can attest to. So I began to wonder what folks meant when they said, "You're looking good."

I think that some people just naturally expect someone with AIDS to look like death, so the fact that I'm looking and acting alive is "looking good." Other people are having a difficult time dealing with all the sickness and death in this epidemic and for them my "looking good" is at once a denial of all the pain in their lives and a hope that maybe things aren't really as bad as they fear. Even those who honestly do believe that I'm looking good have a desire for me to be feeling equally good. And so their next question is inevitably: What are you doing?

I, being a people pleaser and not wanting to disappoint them and having long ago bought into the Puritan Work Ethic, would dutifully respond with a long and detailed list of all the things I was doing: celebrating Mass and the sacraments, preaching, giving spiritual direction, visiting the sick, working on a book—this book, as a matter of fact—giving retreats, and adding whatever current projects might be on my calendar for that week.

Despite the fact that I am technically medically retired, I am busier than I've ever been in my life. Retirement often seems like a fantasy. My involvement in the AIDS epidemic could be written up in an impressive resumé worthy of any two full-time jobs. Since 1981 when I visited the first AIDS patient in San Francisco, I have visited people with AIDS in the hospital and at home bringing the hope of God's love, the consolation of the Sacraments of the Church, and the support of human compassion. I facilitated support groups for lovers and friends who had lost someone to AIDS. I was involved in a coalition of grief support organizations who worked to develop an organized response to the growing level of grief in the Bay Area. I was a member of the AIDS Interfaith Network and then the San Francisco Interfaith Coalition. I have been a volunteer with Shanti, Kairos House, and Dignity. I have done AIDS education with high school- and college-age students, clergy, hospital chaplains, and church groups in a variety of Christian denominations. I did AIDS consciousness-raising with television, radio, newspapers, and magazines. I participated in fund-raising, speaking for United Way, donating money and time. I developed a retreat for persons affected by HIV, gathered a team, and successfully gave the retreat three times. I was invited by the mayor of San Francisco to give him input about how the city might better respond to the epidemic. I participated as a subject in drug trials testing oral Ganciclovir as a treatment for CMV retinitis. I have been "attorney in fact" taking the responsibility to make medical decisions for friends who might lose the capacity to make their own choices as their disease progresses. I have officiated at funerals and memorial services too numerous to count and tried to console grieving friends and family members.

Not bad, I would say, for somebody who's supposed to be retired.

Then one day something changed. I wish I could tell you what happened to make it different but I honestly don't remember. Maybe I looked in the mirror one morning and realized that how I looked and what I did weren't really important. Maybe I just heard for myself what I had been telling so many other people for an awfully long time, that who they are is much more important than what they do. Or, maybe it was a bad day, like today, when my energy is very low and it's very hard to do anything at all. Whatever caused it, I found myself answering the question, "What are you doing?" by saying, "Living one day at a time."

I'm still busy doing things. I guess that's part of my nature, but it's not all that important anymore. Just being is what's important. And for right now, that's a wonderful place to be.

I'm getting better every day,

Bobby

6 February 1990

Dear D,

Last night I watched a PBS special on the influence of the song "We Shall Overcome" on peace, justice, and liberation movements throughout the world. I had seen this particular show before and cried. Last night was no exception; I cried again.

Why do I cry when I hear this song? Is it the power of the simple melody connected to the Negro spirituals as a source of hope in their slavery? Is it the memory it evokes of freedom marches, the Rev. Dr. Martin Luther King, Jr., and the struggle of black people for equality in our land? Is it the waste of life and the death of the "American Dream" that the Vietnam War brought to my generation? Is it the grief of having five friends die in the last four weeks, only adding to the growing number of friends and acquaintances who have or are dying of AIDS?

Are my tears shed in sorrow that our world remains imperfect or that I am too imperfect to change it? Do I cry at the injustice that permits trillion-dollar budgets to coexist with homeless, hungry, jobless people in our own country? Does the song make me cry for the poor in the Third World who struggle to survive war, famine, sickness, while we waste and abuse the resources of the world? Am I crying that the "someday" for overcoming poverty, prejudice, oppression, greed, sickness, and fear is not "today"?

Or could it be that my tears are tears of joy? Could the words and music of "We Shall Overcome" touch a chord of hope deep within me? As I face death, my own and that of many others, do I perhaps cry in solidarity with a humanity both dying and rising, sinful and saved, diseased and healed, poor and rich in those things that really matter: faith, hope, and love?

Maybe why I'm crying doesn't really matter. Maybe the important thing is that I'm crying . . . and in the crying I'm feeling . . . and in the feeling I'm becoming more aware of my oneness with all people, with all creation, with all the dying and the living, with the Source of Life. Maybe my tears are expressing something so deep within me that it defies explanation, an experience of the Oneness of the Universe crying out in pain and in hope:

We shall overcome, someday.

I'm getting better every day,

Bobby

BILL BARCUS: ANOTHER PRIEST
FRIEND DIES

On the Occasion of the Funeral of the
Reverend Canon William Barcus III

19 March 1990

Dear D,

I'm feeling melancholy tonight. I tried to call you
but, since I couldn't reach you, I decided to put my
thoughts on paper so that once again, I could share
them with my favorite listener.

I attended a funeral today. My friend the Reverend Canon William Barcus III (isn't that an impressive name?) of the Episcopal Church died of
AIDS and was buried from Grace Cathedral in San
Francisco this afternoon. It was an impressive cer-
emony, as the Anglican Church is want to do. The
bishop of California celebrated the Mass and gave
the eulogy. The place was filled with people, and a full
choir sang traditional hymns of glory. There were
many familiar faces, priests and laypeople from the
Episcopal Church that I have worked with or been
friends with over the years. There were some no-
table missing faces, too, people that I haven't heard
from for a while. As always, I wondered if maybe

they were sick, or maybe even dead and I hadn't heard. In San Francisco these days with the plague raging, that's always a possibility.

Anyway, let me tell you about Bill. He had been a priest in the Episcopal Diocese of California for many years, having come to the ministry after a successful business career. Bill was a tireless worker, known in San Francisco not so much for his AIDS work, though he did lots of that, but for his advocacy for the homeless and the poor. He even started a shelter for the homeless in the South of Market area. That's a funny story in itself since the building he used had been one of the most active gay bathhouses in the city until they were all closed because of the epidemic.

Bill was an old friend. We had met soon after my arrival in San Francisco and had maintained contact in a variety of ways over the years. He was diagnosed with AIDS ahead of me and survived over five years after diagnosis. Poor Bill was very sick for a long time, experiencing lots of the opportunistic infections like CMV and PCP and KS and some others that I can't even pronounce, one after another or at the same time. All that time he was an angry man, angry at a world that would not accept him fully as a gay man, angry at the Church that in his mind never did enough in the fight against AIDS, angry at the disease and the slowness of the research and the medical profession to move ahead and save more lives. His anger consumed him. Some people thought the anger had kept him going and kept him alive. But since I approach the whole thing from a different perspective, I wonder if the anger didn't really eat him up in the end.

I do want to tell you about what stands out in my mind as one the major moments in which Bill was actually the instrument that made my having AIDS a call to ministry for me. Actually, it was on the night I was diagnosed. We had previously made plans to have dinner that particular night, never expecting that the dinner conversation would include my own diagnosis from that very morning. You can imagine that it was a sad and heavy evening. I almost canceled but decided that since Bill had been living with AIDS more than a year at that point, he might have something to share with me about my situation. I remember that we ate at an Italian restaurant on Castro Street and that soon into the meal we were both crying into our spaghetti. I will never forget the message that Bill gave me that night. He looked at me in my pain and confusion and he said, "Bob, you and I are priests. We both know that lots of people get ordained, but we are priests, and in our priesthood, we want to share with and be with and minister to our people. And our people, yours and mine, are dying of AIDS. You and I could never just stand by and watch them die. We must take their hand and walk the road with them." That very instant, despite all of the confused and mixed emotions I was experiencing, his words gave my AIDS diagnosis a purpose. I will always be grateful to Bill for his counsel that night.

As we both progressed in our illness, I didn't see Bill very often. Usually he didn't want to see anybody, and in his anger he would be very cross or short with people. Interestingly, that never happened with me. I remember running into him at a restaurant one day when he looked particularly bad.

I went over to him (a little gingerly, I must admit, aware of his abrasiveness) and said hello. To my surprise I got a smile. He said he wasn't doing very well . . . but that was nothing new. As we chatted, I worked up enough courage to say, "Bill, I need to ask you something. I know that there are times when you're not feeling well, and you're angry or short with people, and yet you're never that way with me. How come?" He looked at me and said, "I can't be angry at you. You told the truth, you weren't afraid to say who you were to the world. All I can do is respect you for that." I need to tell you how much I respected Bill Barcus for his willingness to stand up and speak his truth.

Well, D, rather than leave you on this somber note, let me tell you something else Bill did that I'll never forget. One Christmas, I received this very fancy Christmas greeting that shows another side of Bill Barcus. Embossed on a very fancy card was this message: "In the prolonged absence of Miss Tallulah Bankhead, the Reverend William Barcus III announces the birth of our Lord."

Good night D,

I am getting better every day,

Bobby

DEPRESSION

14 April 1990

Dear D,

As I write this I'm experiencing a deep and dark depression. This is nothing new. No matter how positive and upbeat I am most of the time, there are times when a darkness comes over me whose origin I can't explain but whose power to bring me down can't be denied or easily put aside. This one has lasted more than a week already. The real bad ones are always this long or longer. I'm noticing some pattern to them now. They seem to come every five to six months, last long enough to make me frightened and miserable, and then they go away.

When I try to analyze them (and I always do even though I know at some deeper level that analysis won't fix it), there is always some very logical, concrete reason for my being depressed. For instance, there have been a number of deaths in the last two weeks both of my friends and my family. Living in San Francisco in 1990 is like living in a war zone anyway, but when dying happens closer to home it just seems to magnify the ongoing experience of grief that never seems to go away.

Then there's the fact that I'm coming on my third anniversary of diagnosis. Since I was originally given a seventeen-month prognosis, I suppose that having survived for three years should be reason to celebrate. But it's been three years of waiting for the proverbial "other shoe" to drop, three years of watching friends and acquaintances die, three years of dealing with family, church, friends, the media, three years of choosing every day to live. Don't get me wrong, it hasn't been all drudgery. In fact, it's been the most life-filled, growth-filled, grace-filled time in my life. But right now I'm sitting in the darkness of depression, and from this perspective I've got some pretty good reasons to be tired and angry.

The physical pain seems somehow more than I can bear. Whether it's the mouth pain with sores like raw hamburger between my gum and lips, on my tongue, and down my throat (sores that make it painful even to drink water), or the diarrhea twenty days out of the month that makes it difficult to walk down the street, fearful that I'll have an accident and be embarrassed. There are days when I have no energy, when I feel like a wet dishrag, and it's hard to even get out of bed.

And besides the physical pain, there's the emotional pain of living every day with a death sentence, of never knowing whether I'll be hurting or OK today, of wondering if today will be the day that some opportunistic infection will take my life. There's the emotional pain of losing friends one after another, over a hundred at this point; the pain of sometimes feeling like a leper; the pain of being afraid. Add to all that the funk induced by all the medicines and drugs that I take. The depressions, the mood swings, what does it all mean? What is the meaning of my life? Why do I even care? Oh, I know that I'm not alone, that I have lots of friends to love and who love me and I know that their support is encouragement to live one day at a time. But today, right now, even that single day seems too difficult to bear. Today I need to live a minute at a time.

In this darkness I can understand those who have lived in the darkness and with the pain long enough and who choose to end it. But understanding doesn't mean agreeing or making that same choice. I guess I'm not yet in total darkness. Maybe I can see a glimmer of light, or maybe I can just remember that there is light somewhere, so in the midst of the darkness and depression, right now, I can still choose to live.

Even at times like this when it's hard to believe it,

I am getting better every day,

Bobby

20 May 1990

Dear D,

Do you remember my telling you how exercising my pastoral priestly ministry, especially in the celebration of Mass and the anointing of the sick, has been personally a healing experience for me? Nowhere was this brought home to me in a stronger way than when I celebrated Mass at the drug trials.

I was in the hospital overnight as part of a study for oral Ganciclovir. That's one of those exotic drugs developed in and around the AIDS epidemic to deal with cytomegalovirus (CMV) with which I am infected. I had to be in the hospital overnight so that they could take blood from me every hour to test it. While I was there, my friend Ed, a nurse who was conducting the tests, came and said, "Bob, how about if after I get off work tonight I stop by with some bread and some wine and you celebrate Mass for us?" Well, you know how I love celebrating Mass and how, because of lots of circumstances, I don't get to do it as often as I'd like. So I jumped at the chance.

Right on schedule after his work shift was done, Ed arrived with bread and wine and we set up for

Mass on the tray table in the hospital room. We read together the word of God which said, "Unless you eat the flesh of the Son of Man and drink his blood, you'll have no life in you." We shared with one another what those words meant to each of us and then we entered into the ancient ritual, "The Lord be with you. . . . Lift up your hearts. . . . It is right that we should give you thanks and praise." And then, I prayed, "On the night before he died for us, Jesus took bread, blessed and broke it and shared it with his friends saying, 'This is my body, this is my blood of the new and eternal covenant.'"

The power of those words led me to remember the first time that I had really understood their whole meaning. It was a long time ago, just two days after my ordination. All the folks that had come for the celebration and the party were getting ready to go back home. And so before they left, they all came to my parents' house one more time for me to celebrate Mass and to have lunch all together. As I celebrated Mass in the living room of my parents' home, I remember getting to the consecration and realizing, maybe for the very first time, what the words meant. I was saying this is *my* body given for you, this is *my* blood poured out for you. I remember I froze. The folks giggled a bit and thought the new priest lost his place. I hadn't lost anything. I was gripped with fear because I realized for the first time what being a priest meant. It was *my* body and *my* blood on the line! And then the next instant I did the only thing I could do in my fear—continue the ritual and the words that followed. It made me understand. "Whenever you do this, remember me." I was not alone, but with these people and every

person with whom I'd celebrate the sacred mysteries, I was sharing in the dying and the rising of
Jesus.

The effects of that lesson learned so long before
were not lost on me on this day when with my friend
Ed in my hospital room we shared once again in the
mystery of the body and blood of Jesus. Only this
day a new insight was added. For here at the drug trials, it was literally my blood that was being poured
out. It was literally my flesh that was being given
for those others, for my sisters and brothers with
AIDS and HIV infection. And as we sat quietly after
communion with the blood of Jesus flowing in our
veins it was Ed who pointed out the goodness of
God, who in the midst of this horrible epidemic
would reveal to us once again in a very practical way
the incredible power of His love.

I have been given the gift to see grace in the face
of sickness and death. I pray for the ability to help
others see.

I'm getting better every day,

Bobby

22 June 1990

Dear D,

Today I celebrated the funeral of yet one more friend. His name was Dan Turner, and until his death a few days ago, he was the longest AIDS survivor, having been diagnosed over seven years ago.

I'd met Dan through our mutual AIDS involvements and had gotten to know him over the years. Because he was a well-known figure in the AIDS world, Dan's funeral was held at Grace Cathedral in San Francisco. I presided wearing the great silver cope that had once belonged to Bishop James Pike. You might remember him as the controversial Episcopal bishop of California who one day simply walked out into the California desert, never to be seen or heard from again.

I was energized as I always am when I lead people in prayer. But tonight those feelings have turned to depression as I realized that I have no place to celebrate Mass. It's true that I have some places where I'm welcome to concelebrate. But what I'm talking about is the feeling of being a preacher without a pulpit, a minister without a congregation, a priest without his people. I continue to be a priest in good standing with the Church and I'm seen as a leader in the gay community. I've defended my right to be both priest and gay. But now I feel like I'm paying the price for telling the truth about myself.

When I went public with my AIDS diagnosis three years ago, in a sense I came out of two closets. I told the Catholic Church that I was gay, which put me at odds with the Church's moral teachings and didn't make me very popular with some of the bishops. And I told the gay community that I was a priest. You know that the Church isn't very popular in the gay community for all of its anti-gay and homophobic stands. So here I am in the middle, too gay for the Church and too Catholic for the gays.

My own experience of ministry tells me that when people's needs call the priesthood out of me, I am given life and healing. The best sermons I preach are always to myself. My friend Ken keeps saying that I'm a priest looking for his parish. I guess I haven't found a particular parish yet that needs or wants all my gifts, but I know that there are many individuals out there who need to hear the message that they are loved and forgiven. For the freedom to proclaim that message I'll put up with having no place to celebrate Mass.

I love you very much and

I'm getting better every day,

Bobby

15 July 1990

Dear D,

I was cleaning out a box of books stored for fifteen
years in my parents' cellar when I found it. *Stella
Matutina* the cover announced. The name means
"Morning Star" and the publication was my grad-
uation yearbook from St. Thomas Seminary in 1966.
A mixture of curiosity and nostalgia led me to get
comfortable and take a trip back in time.

This was a paperback version of the yearbook
intended for personal use, and mine was filled
with autographs beside each of the pictures of
the graduates of 1966. I remember that we also
had a fancy hardbound copy that hadn't survived
my many moves. It seemed strange to look back at
all those young faces with whom I had spent my
nineteenth and twentieth years. I found that while
they looked familiar, at least half evoked no name
as I played a personal game to see how many I
could remember.

St. Thomas was a high school and junior-college
seminary to which I had been sent by my diocese

for the first two years of college. Students came from all over the East Coast to study Latin, Greek, chemistry, modern languages, and to see if maybe God was indeed calling them to the priesthood in the Roman Catholic Church. My memory of the place is sketchy and filled with images of events and situations that might well be titled: "Vignettes in the Quest to Grow Up." But it's the emotional-memory, the feelings that survived half my lifetime, that surprised me by their power and intensity as I paged through the *Stella Matutina*.

Struggle and self-doubt are the first emotional-memories to surface. I recall the difficulty of trying to re-adapt to American culture after four years of high school in a French-Canadian seminary. I could still feel the loneliness and pain of being the "fat kid" who was so easy to pick on, and who was the brunt of jokes that left me feeling ridiculed and devalued. The name *Cheeks* jumped up at me from the pages and, after all these years, still had the power to sting like an old war wound that hurts in bad weather and is a constant reminder of old battles lost or won. It was a nickname I'd been given in high school, probably because of my corpulence and the prominence of that part of my anatomy at both ends of my body. It symbolized for me all the pain that being fat all my life had caused me, all the jokes and cruel remarks, all the rejection and alienation for not being good in sports, all the hatred I'd developed for those four cheeks and the rest of the body that went with them.

How strange, I thought, that after all these years a name and a few pictures could still evoke such powerful feelings. It hurt to remember how unloved, unpopular, and unappreciated I had felt, how disconnected to the Class of 1966 and to myself.

Then I started to read what the Class of 1966 had written in my *Stella Matutina*. "Great guy." "Wonderful smile." "An inspiration in your dedication to the priesthood." "I couldn't have made it through these two years without you." "Your faith and sense of humor will be an asset to the priesthood." "Keep smiling, as you always did here through rough times, and your future success is guaranteed." "Your kindness and charity encouraged me to try harder to love." "You're OK."

Wow! What a surprise to learn that those guys, twenty-five years ago, loved and respected me. I had always thought that no one noticed who I was (except to make some wisecrack about my weight) and worse, that no one cared. How come I didn't know back then how people felt about me? Why hadn't I felt their love . . . even when they'd written it down?

I took a prayer break and thanked God for yet another surprise gift: the healing of the twenty-year-old Bob. And I praised the God of compassion who watches over fools and children.

In the pages of the *Stella Matutina*, a quarter-century old, I'd learned some important lessons: self-acceptance and self-worth only come to us when we are ready to receive them; it's easy to fool ourselves into seeing or believing a lie, even when the truth is spelled out for us in black and white; who I am today has a profound effect on seeing and understanding who I was and who I can become. My belief in a God of Surprises was again reaffirmed!

By the way, some of those guys from St. Thomas Seminary remain to this day cherished and loving friends.

Speaking of loving friends, you rank high on my list. Know that I love you and that

I'm getting better every day,

Bobby

NEW SHOES

10 August 1990

Dear D,

Today I went out and bought a new pair of shoes. They're really nice shoes, all black leather with little gold-colored buckles at the top.

Now, you may be wondering why I'm writing to you about my new shoes. Well, it's not to prove that I'm thrifty, although the shoes were on sale, nor to point out with any kind of fashion statement what a great dresser I am. But you should know that these are the first shoes I have bought since I was diagnosed with AIDS.

I needed new shoes, the other ones were wearing out. But I just hadn't gotten around to buying any. It got me wondering whether all the talk I've been doing about living was only a good line. For over two years now, I've been telling people that "I'm getting better every day," but I wonder if way deep down inside I was convinced that sometime—sooner than later—I was going to die. And so, I couldn't bring myself to buy shoes that I'd never wear out.

Well, today, pushed by the discomfort of holes in my shoes, or by the fact that I've got a lot of walking and living to do, I went out and bought some new shoes. It's just another little victory for living here and now, a day or a shoe at a time, and being the drama queen I am, I had to write and tell you.

I am getting better every day,

Bobby

YOU DON'T KNOW WHO I'VE BECOME

Connie is one of four cousins I grew up with.
This letter to her is really to all of them.

22 October 1990

Dear Connie,

I'm back home safe and sound in San Francisco. I'm using today to rest and to catch up on some long overdue letter writing. I hope that you are dealing as best you can with the death of our cousin Paul. It has been a tough year for the family with Nancy dying in January, Alfred in March, and now Paul in October. I could sense the loss and the pain when "the cousins" gathered for what has become our traditional dinner together. Despite the light-hearted banter and funny stories, something was different. With some of us missing, we are not the same. In fact, we have not been the same close and supportive family for a long time now. That in part is what prompts me to write you this letter. The other part is that given my AIDS diagnosis I fully expected to be dead before any of you. Since I'm still alive, I owe it to myself to take care of this still unfinished business.

First of all, let me tell you that I love you and that I know that you love me. From the time I was a baby you changed my diapers and fought with Jeannette over who would rock me or push me in the stroller. If I was a spoiled brat, all of you spoiled me with all the love and attention you gave me. In that sense we were all spoiled and privileged to grow up in an atmosphere of love. Mémère taught us to be gentle with one another and encouraged us to be more like brothers and sisters than just cousins. Maybe that's why I feel the pain of the distance that has come between us.

There is a natural distancing that growing up and living miles apart creates. But having had the best I cannot be satisfied with less. Since I came home to tell you that I was gay and had AIDS, I have felt you pulling away emotionally and physically. The messages were subtle but clear. Although you knew that I was dealing with the heavy reality of my own death, you did not keep in touch. And when I came home for my yearly visits you never expressed interest or asked me to share any of what was going on with me. The few times I tried to tell you, you changed the subject. I'll bet you are not even consciously aware that since I was diagnosed with AIDS you have never invited me to your house for a visit or a meal like you used to. Instead you've come to visit me at my parents' home, or we've met in a restaurant. I've tried to make excuses to myself saying that you might be afraid of the disease or that you might be angry for what you perceived as my dishonoring the family or hurting my parents. But no excuse could take away the disappointment and hurt I felt when you were not there to support me in the way that you had taught me to expect.

I have received strong support from wonderful friends whose love sustains me in my day-to-day choice for life. Total strangers call me and write to me promising prayers, offering compassion, giving hope. But I'm sad that you, with whom and from whom I learned to love, don't even know who I've become. I'm sure you know the "Bobby" who was like your kid brother or the "Father Bob" who you put on a pedestal and held up for your children's admiration as the "priest of the family." But do you know the part of me that's a hero in the San Francisco gay community for risking to tell the truth about who I am? Do you know the me who reaches out to the sick and the alienated with a message of God's mercy and forgiveness? Do you know how I am stopped regularly on the street by people who say, "Thank you for telling the truth"?

I don't want to be a hero for you or the family any more than I want to be a villain. But I want desperately for you to see me as I am: a whole person, sexual, relational, sometimes powerful, and sometimes dying and afraid.

Please share this with my other cousins: your brother Albert, Jeannette, and Gerry and Doris, too. It is hard enough writing this once. I feel like I am taking a risk in writing this to you. But the risk is taken in hope that we will once again be able to share the special intimacy of our tears and our laughter.

I love you very much and

I'm getting better every day,

Bobby

VISIT TO THE NUNCIO

1 November 1990

Dear D,

I've been meaning to tell you about my visit to the Nuncio, which took place in October of 1990. I hope you're sitting in a comfortable place because this is a fairly long story.

I had gone to Washington, D.C., to visit Damien Ministries. Damien Ministries is a group organized for the care and support of people with HIV. Its founding director, Lou Tesconi, had invited me to Washington to see what they were about and to look at the kinds of ministries they were doing. I had decided that while I was there I would do something that I do very well, shit disturbing. I had planned to go to the offices of the American Bishops Conference to ask them some questions like, How many priests in the United States have AIDS? And what is being done for them? I had also planned to somehow get the message to the Apostolic Nuncio, the papal representative to the country who also resides in Washington and has Ambassadorial status, that there are priests with AIDS living and working and dying in the United States.

My visit with the Damiens was pretty uneventful. I found them to be people who were doing wonderful ministries but who personally were suffering the burnout that often comes from the intense and difficult work of supporting and loving people with HIV.

My visit to the Bishops Conference seemed as if it, too, would be pretty uneventful. The conference offices, a brand new multimillion-dollar complex, are located near the Catholic University of America and within a short walking distance from the Shrine of the Immaculate Conception. As I walked through the marble entryway, I was greeted by a couple of secretaries, receptionists really, at the front office. Both these young women were black, and as I was to find out later, both deeply spiritual though neither one was Roman Catholic. I'm including these details of race and religion because they were important to me as the story unfolded putting these two women in contrast to the other folks, especially the Roman Catholic sisters that I encountered on my visit.

Having introduced myself to the receptionists, I told them I had come to make some inquiries about AIDS among the clergy in the United States and asked if they could recommend someone with whom I could speak. I was referred to a sister on the third floor, and they rang her office. When I spoke with the sister over the house phone, she declined to come down and meet with me, but instead told me she had no information and the priest that did was away in Rome at a meeting and wouldn't be back for a month. After a less than satisfactory telephone conversation, I realized that the folks at the National Bishops Conference were even less willing to deal with the whole issue of AIDS than I had suspected before.

At that point one of the two receptionists asked me why I was asking these questions. I candidly told them that I was a priest living with AIDS and that it was important for me to know how other priests in different parts of the country were being treated. I also told them that I had suspicions about great numbers of priests being affected by AIDS and being too frightened to tell anyone about it. I was hoping to get some information in order to provide them with some support through the Bishops Conference.

The receptionists seemed very moved by my story and one of them offered to take me on a tour of this magnificent building, which I accepted readily. As we walked along the plush carpeted corridors and looked into the magnificent conference rooms and chapels and offices, she asked me lots of questions about what it was like to have AIDS and showed deep compassion, not just for me, but for all people touched by this horrible epidemic. She shared how she was aware of many cases of AIDS in the Washington, D.C., area, and also shared that at least from her vantage point she had experienced very little concern or activity around AIDS from the Bishops Conference.

As we toured the offices of the Catholic News Service she even went out of her way to introduce me to some of the reporters there, but they didn't seem to think that there was any real news in a priest with AIDS. After showing me all around (this was undoubtedly the fifty-cent tour and not the nickel one), we returned to the main entrance.

Before I left, she asked me where I was headed next. I told her that I was looking for some way to tell my story at the Apostolic Nunciature. That's the home and office of the Papal Pro-nuncio to the United States.

She said, "Oh, wait a minute," handed me a telephone, and said, "Call this number." When I did, someone answered at an inside line saying, "Vatican Embassy, may I help you?" I asked if I could speak to one of the priest secretaries. I was told that a Father Tim was on call but wasn't available at the moment, and was asked to call back in about an hour. As I left the offices of the Bishops Conference I was moved by the guarantee of prayers from these two young ladies at the desk. They had both gone out of their way to make me feel welcome and to give me some help and support in accomplishing my goals. With neither ecclesiastical title nor authority, these two women had really been signs of Jesus' love and care.

When I called the Nunciature about an hour later, Father Tim answered the phone. He is one of the four American priest secretaries who work full-time with the Papal Nuncio. He greeted me warmly, saying, "My name is Tim. What can I do for you, Bob?" I told him that I was a priest in good standing, that I was living with AIDS, and that I would welcome an opportunity to come and share some of my story with him in the hope that he would find a way to pass it on to the Nuncio himself. Tim said that he would be very happy to meet with me and to listen to my story, but he felt that perhaps the newly arrived Nuncio, Archbishop Augustino Cachiavillan, might be interested in meeting with me himself.

This was an incredible surprise. Now, you have to understand the Apostolic Nuncio is not only the Vatican's Ambassador to the United States, he is also the top-ranking bishop in the country and the pope's personal representative. To meet with him, even for bishops and archbishops, is the closest thing to having a papal audience. Never in my wildest dreams did I hope to meet with the Papal Nuncio. Father Tim told me that he would pass on the information of my willingness and availability to the archbishop, and we set up a time and place where he would call me back.

At 5:30 sharp that afternoon the phone rang.

"Bob, this is Tim," he said. "I spoke to the archbishop and he's very sorry that his schedule will not allow him to meet with you, but he would like to speak to you by phone and is available right now. Would you be willing to speak with him?"

"Of course," I said. "I'd be honored." In a moment a voice came on the other end of the phone heavy with an Italian accent.

"Father *Arpeen*," he said.

"Yes, your excellency," I said, "but it's French."

"Ahh, Father Arpin."

I said, "Yes."

He said, "What can I do for you?"

My response was immediate. "Absolutely nothing, Archbishop. I am just so honored to have the opportunity to speak with you in person. I had hoped through Father Tim to be able to share with you a little bit of my priestly heart and to tell you what it's like to be a priest with AIDS in the United States."

There was silence at his end of the phone, almost thirty seconds of silence, which is an eternity when you are waiting at the other end of the line. And I must admit I thought to myself, "I blew it."

But then he said to me, "Father, I think we should meet in person. Would you do me the kindness of coming to visit me tomorrow morning at my home?"

"Of course," I said.

At which point he said, "Eleven o'clock, then. I look forward to meeting you."

I hung up the phone and stood there for a moment with my mouth open, surprised at the turn of events.

The next morning I took a taxicab to the Apostolic Nunciature. That's the official name of the Vatican Embassy. It's on Massachusetts Avenue on Embassy Row, almost directly across the street from the vice-president's house. As we drove up the elegant circular drive, I could see the papal Coat of Arms over the front door. A little nervous, I rang the bell and was greeted by a lovely young woman in her twenties dressed very simply. I don't know if she was a secretary or a nun, but most of the nuns that serve the Vatican are in habits. She wasn't.

I was escorted through a couple of formal rooms to a third that had twelve-foot-high ceilings, plush deep-red carpeting, and bigger than life-size oil portraits of former popes with no less formidable figures than Leo the XIII and Pius the IX, both of happy memory, looking down on me. I sat waiting for the Nuncio. His excellency, Archbishop Cachiavillan, presented a much less formal picture than his opulent surroundings. He was a short, slight man. He wore a finely cut but simple Italian suit, had a small amethyst ring with no sign of chain or pectoral cross. I was greeted with a firm but gentle handshake.

"Father Arpin," he said.

"Yes, your excellency. It's a pleasure to meet you," I said.

"Is your first name Albert?" he asked.

"No, your excellency. It's Robert."

"Ahh . . . Bob. May I call you Bob?"

After that the conversation seemed relaxed and easy. I was able to share a good bit of my story with him, answering questions about how it was that I was living and working in California while my diocese was still in Massachusetts. He asked me how close I was to Jesus and if I was able to celebrate Mass every day. I shared with him how important it was for me to be able to exercise my priesthood, especially in my illness, and how the administration of the sacraments brought me great healing.

He shared that he had been sent to the United States from a post as Apostolic Nuncio to India where, in great contrast to this country, he had lived in the midst of sickness and poverty. He seemed to be personally acquainted with Mother Teresa of Calcutta and spoke of her with great reverence. "I have so much to learn about your vast and wonderful country," he said. "Will you please pray for me? I know that God will hear your prayers."

I asked him if in his ministry to the bishops of the United States he might have the opportunity to remind them that first and foremost they should be priests, ministering the mercy and compassion of Jesus. He said of course he would do that. That that also was the mind of the Holy Father. He asked me about my parents and whether I had any brothers and sisters.

When the conversation and visit seemed to be coming to a natural close, he stood and I asked him for his blessing, which he graciously gave me in English. That somehow surprised me, I guess I expected him to do it in Latin. With his arm around my shoulder, he walked me to the magnificent front door of the Nunciature.

There he said, "May I ask you for another favor?"

"Of course, Archbishop," I said. "What can I do for you?"

"I will ask you to bring the Apostolic blessing to your good parents and to your bishop from me, and make sure to tell your bishop that I send you with the Apostolic blessing."

I ended my visit with the Nuncio with the feeling that I'd really been heard and that here was a person who despite his exalted office and grave responsibilities had cared enough to take the time to listen to the heart of an ordinary priest.

I did, of course, carry the archbishop's blessing to my parents and my bishop in Springfield. When I shared the story of my visit to the Nuncio with a friend of mine who is also a bishop in San Francisco, his eyes lit up and he asked me if I realized what the archbishop had done. "By sending you to your bishop with the Apostolic blessing, he was sending a clear message that you had his blessing and that you are OK."

That made the whole thing even more special.

I guess I was in the right place at the right time again. I must have some guardian angel watching over me. Why not? I have good friends like you and that, too, is a miracle.

I am getting better every day,

Bobby

1991

14 February 1991

Dear D,

God has to have a great sense of humor. Among the many stories I've heard illustrating this—beyond my own life story—is this one that I want to share with you. I wish I could take credit for it, or even give credit to whoever wrote it, but I honestly don't know who did.

It seems there was a God-fearing, Bible-reading man who lived on a farm in the land of Nowhere Special. One day in Ordinary Time rains came, floods followed, and the man was in fear of his life. So he climbed onto the roof of his house to get away from the raging water, and there he prayed to God to save him. While he was praying, some people came by in a rowboat and offered him a place in it, but he continued praying, saying, "God will save me." A while later when the waters were rising even higher, a helicopter came by and lowered a ladder for him to climb in. But he waved them away saying, "God will save me." Well, as you might guess, the man drowned. And because God is patient and merciful, he was taken up to heaven. But when he came face-to-face with God, he was angry and said, "God, why did you let me down? I believed in you and trusted you, but you never came to save me." And God said, "My son, I sent you a rowboat and a helicopter. Wasn't that enough?"

There have been times in my life—like when I was diagnosed with AIDS or when I discovered that I was gay six months after ordination—when I felt like someone caught in a flood with raging water rising up to drown me. Like the man in the story, I, too, prayed to God to save me. In God's own time and God's own way someone came along or something unexpected happened to save me despite myself. Thank God I am learning that God is full of surprises. In that light I wonder if maybe I should reconsider the story of my life. Maybe what I thought were threatening floodwaters are just the way life is. And maybe for me, being gay and having AIDS were in fact God's way of rescuing me from drowning in partial truths and mediocrity and fear. I'm glad God has a sense of humor. That way God can laugh with me instead of at me.

I'm getting better every day,

Bobby

31 March 1991

Dear D,

Happy Easter!
I seem to be spending lots of time lately reviewing past events in light of the present. In my attempt to live one day at a time I try to see each person and event of my life as a gift. And so I'm remembering a time when, although precious, people in my life were few.

Easter of 1976 found me living on my own for the first time ever in my own apartment. I used the occasion to throw a party. I wish I could say my motives were to celebrate the resurrection of Christ or even the return of the Easter Bunny. But in all honesty, the driving forces for throwing the party were loneliness and fear.

I had arrived in San Francisco at Thanksgiving, having driven across the country from Massachusetts, as the first stage in a long journey of self-discovery. What I discovered was that good jobs were hard to come by and that doing the right thing could be very lonely and painful.

By Easter I'd managed to make acquaintance with twenty people. I decided to invite all of them to the party, thinking that even if just one or two showed up, I at least would not spend Easter alone. I remember that I baked a ham, deviled some eggs, and even made some old-fashioned bread and eggs cooked in maple syrup like my grandmother used to. To my great surprise and delight all twenty people showed up, and we all had a wonderful time.

Now, fifteen years later, I remember those twenty people and look back at the events of that day. Two of the people who met for the first time at my party established a relationship that lasted more than a dozen years. Some of the folks that were there are dead now. Others I have completely lost touch with. And some others continue to share my life journey. But every one of those twenty people who came to the Easter party in 1976 helped to teach this lonely and frightened young man in search of himself that maybe . . . just maybe . . . he was worth knowing and being friends with. And for that lesson, and that friendship, I am grateful even to this day.

Maybe it's time to have another party to celebrate the miracle of each moment in our lives and the fact that

I am getting better every day,

Bobby

16 May 1991

Dear D,

I was talking to a priest on the phone the other day. I guess that's not surprising considering my profession, but this was a priest that I hadn't talked to or seen in a couple of years. He had asked about my health, and I was sharing that the disease was progressing and that I'd come home to say good-bye.

"You've got a lot of guts, kid," he said.

Well, I didn't feel particularly brave and so I said, "No more than anybody."

And he said, "Listen to me. You certainly do. You're very brave. I couldn't do it."

That got me thinking about bravery. Is it brave to accept reality? My sense of bravery had always been war heroes or someone who risked his or her life to save someone else. I certainly didn't feel like that kind of hero, but I liked hearing what he said. It made me feel good to be acknowledged . . . to get stroked.

Then I started to think about my friend Bob. Bob is an addict and a person living with AIDS. A

couple of years ago his life was going down the toilet. He was slowly killing himself with IV drugs and
telling himself that it did not matter . . . that his
life was not worth saving. That's when he got sick.
It's funny what can happen to you when you find out
you are going to die. Faced with the reality of AIDS,
Bob chose to live. He started going to NA meet-
ings. He cleaned up his life, eliminating unhealthy
people as well as things. He began taking care of
himself as if he really mattered. Eventually he even
began to help others on their road to wholeness.
Recently Bob fulfilled a lifelong dream to go to
Holland and see the tulips in bloom. Bravery comes
in all shapes and sizes.

   I wonder if they give medals for living one day at
a time.

                              I'm getting better every day,

                              Bobby

27 June 1991

Dear D,

Gay Pride Day and I'm sitting in the hospital. I've been here for a week fighting an infection that got me seriously dehydrated and too weak to walk. So as this city celebrates with a parade and party, I decided to send to you, my friend and confidant, my own statement of pride.

I am gay. It shouldn't surprise you since you've always known that I'm a happy person. Isn't that what gay means? But in case you have any doubt, let me state clearly and without reservation that in my case, being gay means I am homosexual. Emotionally, sexually, and physically I'm attracted to people of the same sex, in this case, to men.

I believe that all sexuality and my sexuality is a gift from God. And since God doesn't make junk, being gay is wonderful. We all need to feel good about ourselves, don't we?

I'm sick and tired of hearing the myths about being gay. One of them is that gay people are sad and lonely and unhappy. What makes me sad is to see people who reject their own sexuality, whatever it is, and refuse to see it as a wonderful, exciting part of their lives. If I'm lonely it's only because people I love go away from me because of their own prejudice and fears. And if I'm unhappy it's because I can't live my life freely as I am because people around me put judgments and strange ideas about who I am in the way.

Lots of theories have been put forth about why people are gay. I frankly don't think it's important, though I will say I don't think it's environmental. After all, both my parents were straight and that didn't rub off on me. Furthermore, I went to Catholic school and was taught by nuns for nine years and never wanted to be a nun. Oh well, maybe just once when I thought it would be fun to wear the habit! And I've lived under Catholic influence all my life, and if what we believe were environmental, I would believe that gays are bad because that's what the Church has been saying. And I don't believe that for a minute.

Some people think being gay is a choice and call it sexual preference. I never met anybody who chose to be heterosexual, so why would being homosexual be a choice? Still other people think it's in the genes. Well, while I've had some cute men in jeans turn my head, I'm sure that didn't make me gay. All that is important is that each of us be the best he or she can be.

While I'm at it, I resent always being lumped with alcoholics or drug users as if my gayness were an addiction, or with child molesters as if gay people were all perverts, or even with diabetics as if being gay was a sickness. But again, I don't want to be lumped with Republicans or Protestants or red-heads either. If you want to put me in a category, put me with those who are lovers, who are compassionate, who believe in God and in themselves, and who try to do the best they can with what they have.

Yes, I'm gay and proud of it! But you already knew that so I guess I wrote this more for myself than for you. It does sound a bit militant . . . but what the hell, it is after all Gay Pride Day.

Even from the hospital I know that I am getting better every day.

Love,

Bobby

15 July 1991

Dear D,

It's raining. In fact, it's been raining all night. Right now it's a soft, gentle, soaking rain. At times during the night it was a driving rain pushed by the wind, hitting the window of my room, or being splashed up from great puddles as an occasional car would drive down the very quiet street.

I didn't used to like rain, but that was before the last five years of drought in California, before experiencing a water shortage so acute that we could only flush the toilet three times a day and we couldn't let the water run to brush our teeth. We had to take five-minute showers, and restaurants even stopped serving water unless you specifically asked for it. Having lived in that drought condition, it's fun to see and hear the rain again coming down like a wonderful gift from heaven to water the land and give it and us life.

Isn't it funny how the lack of something can help you appreciate it more or differently? Remember that old saying, "That guy wasn't smart enough to come in out of the rain." Next time I see someone walking merrily along in the rain, instead of criticizing him, maybe I should wonder if he's been living under drought conditions.

I am getting better every day,

Bobby

28 July 1991

Dear D,

It's a typically hot July afternoon in Western Massachusetts. I'm sitting in the crowded waiting room
of a doctor's office—air-conditioned, thank God—
waiting to meet the doctor. He was referred to me
as a knowledgeable AIDS resource during my two-
month stay here this summer. The office is in the
Spanish-speaking part of town. On the walls are
posters in English and Spanish encouraging people to avoid AIDS, not to share needles, to use con-
doms. The office is bustling with people waiting,
children crying, old people and young people chat-
tering happily away in Spanish, too fast for my un-
trained ear to understand. The room had stopped
and all heads turned to look at me when I came in.
I guess they were surprised to see a priest sitting
there among them. A few smiled, others just look
puzzled.

The whole scene threw me back to a time many
years ago when I first arrived in San Francisco on a
leave of absence. Back then, poor as a church mouse,
I had been reduced to going for public assistance

for help. For the first time in my life I had personally experienced the dehumanizing effects of "the system," standing and waiting in long lines for hours to be given the dole of the state in the form of food stamps or Medi-Cal, which is a California medical insurance for the poor. I was grateful that help was available to me back then. They literally meant the difference to my survival. I remember, with great humility, that first Christmas in California when I was so poor I had nothing to give for Christmas presents. With food stamps I was able to buy the ingredients to bake Christmas cookies, which I hung as ornaments on the small tree I'd gotten and also gave to the few friends I had as a token of Christmas cheer.

For the first time in my life I had experienced what it meant to be poor, really poor, and to be among those folks in ever growing numbers—then and now—who live from minute to minute and day to day, who feel like victims, powerless against what seems to be a negative fate. Reared in a good home, the product of twenty-one years of Catholic education, I had been—until that moment in my thirtieth year—what a priest, who had preached a retreat to us at the seminary years before, had termed a "kept man": kept by family, kept by institutional religion, kept, nourished, fed very well, and supported by Holy Mother Church. I realized then that for the first time in my life, I was completely on my own, dependent on my own resources and those of the state for survival. I learned some important lessons about the meaning of human dignity, about my dignity and that of the other folks who stood in those long, impossible lines waiting for the help that was rightfully theirs. It was for me a real experience of growing, of seeing a side of the world I had never been exposed to and a side of the world that, unfortunately as time went on, would grow in ever greater numbers across our country.

In 1976 I had felt like a victim: powerless and dependent. But now in 1991, even as I remember, I know that I am not a victim anymore. For I had decided to take charge of my life way back then, and now, faced with much greater odds than those as a person living with AIDS, I can still experience my own power, even sitting here sick and waiting for the doctor. Waiting, I have learned, has less to do with power and more to do with the good use of time. As I write this I pray for the people around me. I hope they might know that they, too, have power as they wait to see the doctor.

I am being called . . . have to go. Know that I love you very much and that

I'm getting better every day,

Bobby

10 August 1991

Dear D,

Today is my birthday—forty-five years old! I bet there were times when you wondered if I'd make it. To tell the truth, I did, too. But here I am, and I'm thinking of the birthday—the very special birthday—that you helped me to celebrate when I turned forty.

Forty was a very good age and time for me. I had, in my own estimation at least, paid my dues. I had managed to bring together in balance the major components of my life that were operative at that point. AIDS, of course, had not yet personally entered the picture for me, but as I turned forty, I was successfully balancing being a man, a male of the human species, gay, and a Roman Catholic priest. And so it was logical that I would want to spend my birthday with you folks who had always accepted me just as I am, no questions asked and no unreasonable expectations. With you I was and am always free to be just Bobby. Our love for each other made that possible. Isn't it funny how love is contagious?

I remember how it was when I had told you that I wanted to come to Las Vegas to spend my fortieth birthday with you and you had said: "Wonderful, but we're going to throw you a party." And what a party it was! All of the people there were your friends, most of whom I knew only slightly. But they brought me gifts and cards and bottles of champagne. You hired a bartender and a waitress to serve the wonderful food set up down by the pool. And of course there was the exotic dancer you hired and the X-rated birthday cake that, along with the wonderful people to celebrate with, made my fortieth birthday unforgettable. We must have put on quite a show for that sweet-sixteen birthday party going on at the exact same time at the other end of the same pool! As I think back on it, that party was the celebration of my life to that point.

Today, five years later, I am in a very different place, and the circumstances of my life have changed. This afternoon I will be with my mom and dad to honor my birthday in a much more subdued setting with a homemade pineapple upside-down cake. But I will celebrate my life as it is with no less gusto and no less enthusiasm. I am living it one day at a time, and each day has become a celebration of life and love and truth. I do not know if I'll be around for any more birthdays . . . but I hope to be able to celebrate each and every one of them with a clear sense of who I am and with the closeness and the love of good friends.

Across the miles share a birthday toast with me: May each day be the Birthday of the rest of our lives!

I love you very much and

I'm getting better every day,

Bobby

THE LADY IN THE HOYOKE
GERIATRIC HOSPITAL

28 August 1991

Dear D,

One day a couple of weeks ago I was in the middle of one of my spells. You know the kind, when my energy is so low and I'm so weak that it's hard to drag myself out of bed. I had made a commitment to celebrate Mass at a local geriatric hospital. And so, with great difficulty, I got myself over there. Even with the Deacon to do the readings and preach the homily, I finished Mass counting the minutes when I could get home and back to bed. That's when they told me that an elderly lady was asking to see the priest. I hesitated, took a deep breath, and started out for her room.

On the way I wondered what she might want. It had not seemed like an emergency, but more the need for someone to talk to. And in my current state of low energy that could be difficult. I found her lying on her bed, her hair in place, her clothes immaculate, with frail translucent skin and a lovely smile. The conversation went something like this:

THE LADY: Oh, Hello, Father, I'm so glad you could come. (Her eyes filled up with tears.)

FATHER BOB: (Sitting down now next to her.) Do you want to talk about it?

THE LADY: I don't understand, Father. I don't know what I've done. Why is God punishing me?

FATHER BOB: Now, why do you think you are being punished?

THE LADY: Father, I pray every night and ask God to come and take me, and he doesn't. I'm old and tired. My children are all grown and so are my grandchildren. And they're good kids. And now, I'm just a burden. But hard as I pray, God won't let me die.

It was a familiar story. One I've heard many times before from old people carrying the burden of their years: declining health, living more and more of their lives in the past, and desperately trying to hang on to what is left of their memories. They wonder why on earth God is keeping them around. I've heard the same story from much younger people, too. People burdened with AIDS, with losing their mental and emotional faculties, who wonder why God doesn't come and get them. I had even asked a similar question myself in these past few days when I'd been sick and without energy and wondering if after four long years living with AIDS it wasn't a bit cruel of God to keep me around.

THE LADY: My children really love me, Father, but they don't need me anymore. They don't understand when I tell them I want to die.

(She began crying softly again.) Oh, excuse
me, Father, I guess I've become a real crybaby
in my old age. I cry more now than I ever have.
Oh Father, what's the matter with me?

FATHER BOB: Maybe you're just tired.

THE LADY: Tired, Father?

FATHER BOB: Yes. Tired from all the years of
work and love and life. . . . Do you remember
when you were much younger and your children were still little? I bet there were days way
back then when, as much as you loved them,
you would have loved to hang them all on nails
in the kitchen wall and to tell your husband
that if you had to wash one more dish, or
mend one more shirt or one more sock, you'd
leave it all.

THE LADY: (Looking up at me now with a
smile.) Yes, I remember those days.

FATHER BOB: But you really didn't mean it,
did you? You were just tired. And being tired
brought those kinds of thoughts to your mind.
Maybe right now you're just tired.

THE LADY: I'm old, too, Father. . . and sick.

FATHER BOB: It sounds like all you have to
look forward to is dying.

THE LADY: Oh, yes, what else is there at my
age?

FATHER BOB: There are days (and I was thinking . . . just like today) when I know exactly
how you feel.

THE LADY: You, Father? You're so young.

FATHER BOB: Yes, but age has little to do
with it. I have an incurable disease, and like

you I'm getting ready to face God sooner than later.

THE LADY: But you're so young, and there's so much left for you to do. But what is there left for me to do, Father?

FATHER BOB: I don't know. Maybe God wants you to pray for me.

THE LADY: Do you think so?

FATHER BOB: I know that God works in very mysterious ways. (The lady looked at me with a question in her eyes. I prayed a silent prayer for guidance, took a deep breath, and went on.) I think you and I need to choose to live . . . every day.

THE LADY: To live?

FATHER BOB: Yes. Dying is boring, but living can be exciting. Every day when I wake up and find that God has left me on this earth, I thank God for another day and ask to understand what God wants me to do that day. I try not to think too much about the future, but to live one day at a time.

THE LADY: I think I can live one day at a time.

FATHER BOB: I know you can.

(Before I left, I asked her if I could give her a kiss.)

THE LADY: Of course, I'd love a kiss from a handsome young man.

That kiss made my day!

As I climbed into bed for a well-deserved nap, I thought about the mysterious ways of God who

had told me through this wonderful lady at the geriatric hospital why I should continue living one day
at a time.

I am getting better every day,

Bobby

MY BURIAL PLACE

8 September 1991

Dear D,

You will be glad to know that I have planned my funeral. Or maybe you won't, but I planned it anyway. I
did it on a day when I was sort of down and depressed
and when I was done I felt great! Strange, isn't it? Or
typical for me. In control until the very end.

Speaking of ends . . .

I went to Montreal last week and decided to be
buried in Chicopee, and if that sounds like convo-
luted logic, you're right, it is. I accepted an invitation from an old friend to go to Canada with him
because it would give me the opportunity to spend
some quality time with him on the way and be in
touch with my French-Canadian roots. On both
counts the trip was a resounding success.

But something happened to me along the way. I
decided that when I die, I want to be buried in
Chicopee. I need to tell you that that represents a
major shift in my thinking. I've always said that I
didn't care what anybody did with me after I was
dead, and that if my friends wanted to stuff me and

stand me in the corner, that would be fine. The truth is that I wanted to be cremated and to have my ashes scattered in San Francisco Bay and off the coast of Kauai.

I'm not sure what brought about this change in attitude or why I would now even care what would happen to my mortal remains. Maybe facing my death, or rather reviewing my life, helped me to see what a long and difficult journey I've been on for most of it, so that, at journey's end, I'd want a final resting place. Or maybe I've finally come to see how divided I've been most of my life trying to bring together those disparate parts of myself as a believer, as a gay man, as a person with AIDS, and that now when I'd done a reasonably good job of making peace I didn't want what was left of me scattered like ashes in the wind. Or maybe I just have a need to be remembered, and I'm hoping that as long as that cemetery exists in Chicopee and people come to visit there, they would see my name carved in the stone and remember me.

There is at least one more possibility. My friend Ed tells me that one of the things they are seeing in long-term survivors of AIDS is the development of a homing instinct. That explains why people are searching for a spiritual home and why those that don't find one seem to have this instinct to go back to where they are from, even moving across the country. I guess it's possible that my visit here this summer to my birthplace and my visit to Canada and to my family's French-Canadian roots somehow kicked in my homing instincts and my desire to be buried in the place of my birth.

Anyway, that's the story of how I went to Montreal and decided to have my mortal remains buried in Chicopee. I can only hope that the rest of me will by then have found peace in my true spiritual home.

I'm getting better every day,

Bobby

P.S. A priest friend who is pastor of a parish with a large cemetery has offered me a free plot. However, I don't plan to use it any time soon!

I'VE FOUND PEACE

Brother Roger is the founder of an ecumenical
community dedicated to Christian unity. Their center
in the heart of France's Burgundy country draws
people from all over the world to participate
in their prayer.

Brother Roger
Taizé, France
15 October 1991

Dear Brother Roger,

Today I was in Taizé and had the pleasure of sharing in the noonday prayer with you and the community of people gathered there in faith. My last visit to Taizé was in 1985. At that time, I spent a whole week with the community. This time, unfortunately, it was just a few hours. As before, I was deeply moved by what I experienced: the songs, the prayers, the spirit of reverence, peace, and love of God could be felt in the Church of Reconciliation. There seemed to be more of many things since my last visit, especially more buildings and more people. Only the number of brothers seemed less. I wonder, is that really the case?

One of the songs we sang at prayer on this Feast of Saint Teresa of Avila asked Jesus not to let us hear the darkness that speaks within us. My own experience tells me that when I speak my own truth, courageously and clearly as God gives me to see it, the darkness is silenced by the songs of praise in my heart. And so I need to share with you some of what has happened to me since my last visit to Taizé and how in God's strange and wonderful ways you and the community played a part in the events of my life.

In 1985 I came to Taizé looking for rest, and, like many people who come to you, looking for inner peace. My week here gave me both. As a result I remember inquiring from one of the brothers whether it would be possible to spend more time in the community, perhaps six months or a year. I was told then that that was not possible. The community was not recruiting or seeking new vocations and that while some young people could stay for longer periods of time, adults were discouraged from doing so. Instead I was encouraged to go back and live out my life in my own community and setting.

So I went home and began work with the grieving for the Archdiocese of San Francisco in California. I should tell you that I am a priest with an expertise in hospital ministry.

In April of 1987, just about two years after my visit to Taizé, I was diagnosed with AIDS. Since then my life has changed. I can say without hesitation that AIDS is the greatest gift I have ever received. From the darkness of sickness and fear I saw the light of truth and heard the voice that says, Do not fear, I am with you. I don't know if anything would have been different if I had stayed in Taizé, since I believe that I was infected with the AIDS virus long before 1985. But the advice I received to "go home" put me at diagnosis right in the heart of the AIDS epidemic in the United States where I could receive the best possible care and provide a most needed ministry.

As of now, I'm doing fairly well, thank God. I continue to exercise my ministry as a Roman Catholic priest giving witness to the gay community, to the AIDS community, and to the Church in San Francisco about God's love and boundless mercy. Since at the time of diagnosis the doctors projected that I would live about seventeen months, it is probably safe to say that God is not through with me yet.

In Taizé, six years ago, I had come looking for peace. At prayer in Taizé today, I knew that I had found that peace, not in this place, though it is here, but in the darkness and the light that is within me. As I looked at the many hundreds of young people who had journeyed here, searching for meaning, searching for truth, searching to discover who they are in their world, I knew that there is hope for the world.

I thank you for your efforts in providing a welcome to them and to people like me who pass by on the journey of life. I ask for your prayers and the prayers of your community for me and for all people living with AIDS. May God continue to use us all to proclaim the message of peace and reconciliation in the world.

I'm getting better every day,

Rev. Robert L. Arpin

1 November 1991

Dear D,

Someone asked me recently if I believed in life after death. In response I quoted an infamous priest friend who said: "I don't believe in life after death; I believe in life after life." I am talking about reincarnation. Now I know that the Church has given reincarnation a bad rap. But when I did a little bit of research on the subject, I discovered that the condemnation of reincarnation was orchestrated by the wife of an early Christian emperor who was concerned that some reincarnated imperial ancestor would lay claim to the throne and steal her children's inheritance. Now somehow that does not seem like a very good reason to condemn reincarnation. In concept at least it seems to me to be a very intelligent way of explaining how the universe works. Here is my theory. You can judge it on its own merits.

I think that we all come from God and return to God. Whether that journey takes one lifetime in this world or many is not as important as successfully completing it. Take me for instance. I'm a slow learner and I've probably been around for about five hundred lives. Hopefully, this is one of the last. In any case, as I see it, the time for learning and growth is not in this world, but between lifetimes when we are in school at the feet of the divine teacher. There we learn firsthand what God is like and how we, in our spiritual strivings, can attain to those qualities of divinity.

The time spent embodied in this world is the practicum, the fieldwork, if you will, a time to embody or experience firsthand the lessons that we have learned between lives with God. It seems to me that whole process is very much like people going to school. When you are very little and go to kindergarten you are told what you need to learn because you need the basics: how to get along with others, how to read, how to count. But as you get older and more mature, as you learn more, then you have more say in the planning of your school curriculum so that when you get to graduate school, most of your curriculum is planned by you in conjunction with your teachers. You choose the courses you are going to take, the way you most need to experience them, based on what will best promote the learning that you must do. I think that as people advance in the spiritual realms and become more and more godlike with every incarnation, they have an opportunity to make some significant choices along with God about what they're going to experience in the next lifetime. And so, in conjunction with God, we might even choose when and where we are to be born, who our parents are going to be, what the specific circumstances of our lives will be, and when we will die.

This, it seems to me, is the ultimate explanation of the theory of free will. Not that we are free to choose on a day-to-day level, but rather before we're even born we choose all those events and situations that will most help us to learn the lessons we need to learn in a particular lifetime. This theory of free will would certainly explain how so many things that seem to happen beyond our control are really our free choices. They would also in some ultimate way take away people's responsibility for each other. What happens to me in any given lifetime is my responsibility because I chose it. People have to deal with their own issues. But the ultimate responsibility for my living and dying is mine in conjunction with God.

According to my theory, as I get more advanced and make choices along with God about what I am to experience and how I am to live, it's as if God and I are writing a script to a very elaborate play. Part of the process of being born is to forget the script so that I can approach each event and each situation of my life with a newness and a freshness. After all, if I knew ahead of time how the story was going to end, it wouldn't be half as exciting.

This helps to explain for me the phenomenon known as déjà vu. You know, it's that situation where people get glimpses of things and think, gee, I've done this before, I've been here before. I think that in déjà vu we are remembering little bits and parts of the script we have written and of where our life is supposed to be going.

I also have a theory that we spend eternity in soul clusters. That the same spiritual persons are our closest intimates in each lifetime, in one our parents, in another our children, and in another our lover or our arch rival, but always together, always knowing one another. Have you ever had the experience of meeting someone for the first time, supposedly, and thinking, gee, I can talk to them as if I've known them forever? My guess is you probably have.

I can find no logical reason why my theory couldn't fit into all the beliefs of Christianity. It preserves free will; it preserves God's sovereignty; it preserves the notion that we all come from God and ultimately return to God. It does not deny the goodness of God or the mercy of God. In fact, it supports the reality that at every moment of every day, God is part of our lives and enters into our history.

For me it helps explain lots of unexplainables and answers lots of unanswerable questions. And the fun part is it doesn't really matter because in any case, I must live my life as it is, one day at a time. The only added dimension for me is that this theory says that I have more than one lifetime in which to learn about the divine in me and that ultimately I am saved. But I'm asked to believe that anyway, that I am saved by the mercy and power and the goodness of God.

I used to think that once I died I would have the answers to all of my questions about life and death and afterlife. Now I'm beginning to wonder if maybe once I die and the answers will be available, I won't care. Faced with the reality of the vision of God, who's going to want to know?

I am getting better every day,

Bobby

6 December 1991

Dear D,

Happy Saint Nicholas Day!
With the end of the year rapidly approaching, I am prompted to look back on my life this past year, in fact these past four years that I've been writing to you, and to review the many lessons that living with AIDS has taught me. Don't worry, I don't plan to list them all again and besides, you've already read them and in many cases lived through them with me as my companion on the journey.

If I could put it in a nutshell, it might be *take life as it comes and live it the best you can, one day at a time.*

When I was young I had visions of doing something "special" with my life, maybe even somehow "saving the world." As I got older, but not much wiser, the vision was dulled. I became a bit jaded and began wondering if anyone, including me, could be saved. In facing death and living with AIDS I have come to realize that I can't even save myself, nor do I have to; that is God's job. The best I can do and that which makes me really "special" is simply to be who I am.

In that way my life has been no different from anyone's and my story is everyone's. Except for the infinite variety of details the human story is the same: living and dying, loss and victory, crisis and opportunity. A very wise teacher of mine once told me, "Adversity is like fire; it can reduce you to ash or refine you to gold. It all depends what you're made of." My hope is that when my refining process is over, I will have more than a pile of ashes to show for it.

In the meantime, I have found my visions again, though maybe I'm at an age where they are called dreams. I dream of a world without AIDS, without prejudice, without fear. I dream of a world where everyone and everything exists in harmony and all reflects the divine light.

For now I am living in that light, or trying to, one day at a time. I thank God every morning for the gift of another day and the opportunity to love and be loved. I don't plan to sit around and wait to die. I plan to spend every moment getting ready to live forever. That way, I can honestly say,

I'm getting better every day,

Bobby